ECONOMICS HANDBOOK SERIES

SEYMOUR E. HARRIS, EDITOR

THE AMERICAN ECONOMY

ECONOMICS HANDBOOK SERIES

SEYMOUR E. HARRIS, Editor

ADVISORY COMMITTEE: Edward H. Chamberlain, Gottfried Haberler, Alvin H. Hansen, Edward S. Mason, and John H. Williams. *All of Harvard University.*

The American Economy

ALVIN H. HANSEN
Lucius N. Littauer Professor of
Political Economy, Emeritus
Harvard University

McGRAW-HILL BOOK COMPANY, INC.
New York   Toronto   London
1957

THE AMERICAN ECONOMY

II

To My Wife
MABEL LEWIS HANSEN
for her steadfast devotion
and encouragement

EDITOR'S INTRODUCTION

For years many teachers of economics and other professional economists have felt the need of a series of books on economic subjects which is not filled by the usual textbook, nor by the highly technical treatise.

This present series, published under the general title, *The Economics Handbook Series,* was planned with these needs in mind. Designed first of all for students, the volumes are useful in the ever-growing field of adult education, and also are of interest to the informed general reader.

The volumes are not long—they give the essentials of the subject matter within the limits of a few hundred pages; they present a distillate of accepted theory and practice, without the detailed approach of the technical treatise. Each volume is a unit, standing on its own.

The authors are scholars, each writing on an economic subject on which he is an authority. In this series the author's first task was not to make important contributions to knowledge—although many of them do—but so to present his subject matter that his work as a scholar will carry its maximum influence outside as well as inside the classroom. The time has come to redress the balance between the energies spent on the creation of new ideas and on their dissemination. Economic ideas are unproductive if they do not spread beyond the world of scholars. Popularizers without technical competence, unqualified textbook writers, and sometimes even charlatans control too large a part of the market for economic ideas.

In the classroom *The Economics Handbook Series* will serve, it is hoped, as brief surveys in one-semester courses, as supplementary reading in introductory courses, and in other courses in which the subject is related.

This is the third volume Professor Hansen has contributed to the Handbook Series. His two earlier volumes were *Monetary Theory and Fiscal Policy*, and *Guide to Keynes*; the reader should consult the Editor's Introduction to these volumes for details of his distinguished career.

In the present volume Professor Hansen reviews the economic advances of the last generation and shows how they apply to the policy issues of the recent past, the present, and the near future. The reader will find much rich material on the improved techniques for stabilizing and expanding our economy, and on the relevance of Keynesian economics, now an accepted part of economics even to most of the skeptics of ten to twenty years ago. The book is, incidentally, a vindication of all those who held and developed the theory, in the face of strong opposition, that government has some responsibility for stability and growth; and a reminder of the reluctance with which many, now wedded to the economic theories developed in the last generation, yielded to theories that stressed the importance of the consumption function, liquidity preference, fiscal policy, and the objective of full employment. The volume as a whole reveals the great advances in economic thinking over a generation and the resultant gains in national stability, investment, growth, productivity, and distribution. No American economist has contributed more than Professor Hansen to the advance and dissemination of this part of economics.

In the current volume, Professor Hansen examines the developments of Keynes's thought, the evolution of the President's Council of Economic Advisers, the increased responsibility of government for the economic health of the nation, the relation of rising output and prices, the inadequacies of monetary against fiscal policy—these are among the important issues discussed.

SEYMOUR E. HARRIS

PREFACE

The greater part of this book consists of six lectures given on the Charles R. Walgreen Foundation at the University of Chicago, May 7–18, 1956. Except for the stimulus of the invitation to deliver these lectures this book would probably not have been written. I wish to express my appreciation to the officers of the Foundation, especially to Mr. Jerome G. Kerwin, and also to the members of the Department of Economics at the University of Chicago for the warm reception I received, and to the attentive and stimulating audiences which attended my lectures.

I have added a number of chapters which serve the purpose of expanding somewhat topics which could not be fully developed in the course of the public lectures. I have also added, as an Appendix, a lecture delivered at the Harvard University Memorial Celebration in honor of Woodrow Wilson.

I wish to express my appreciation for the facilities for research and writing made available by the Graduate School of Public Administration of Harvard University, and for the stimulus of association and discussion with members of the Department of Economics.

I am especially indebted to Professor Seymour Harris, the Editor of the Economic Handbook Series, for his careful reading of my manuscript and for detailed criticisms. Also

I am grateful to Mrs. Harvey Andrews for assistance in preparing the manuscript for the printer.

I wish to express appreciation to the *Review of Economics and Statistics*, the *Virginia Quarterly Review*, and the National Planning Association for permission to reprint previously published materials.

ALVIN H. HANSEN

CONTENTS

CHAPTER 1

LOW-PRESSURE VERSUS
HIGH-PRESSURE ECONOMICS [1]

A. Post First World War versus
Post Second World War

Two world wars were fought in the first half of the twentieth century. Both left a terrific impact upon the economic development of the Western world. Both distorted the structure of economic life, shattered established conventions, and destroyed timeworn institutions. Both let loose a flood of problems. The heady wine of revolutionary change had come, and new bottles had to be fashioned.

After the First World War countries tried to pour the new wine into old bottles, but it did not work. The art of inventing new economic institutions is a difficult one. The forces that demanded change were running wild, and no one had yet learned to control them.

There is a vast difference between the economic performance following the First World War and that following the Second World War. Stagnation followed the First; expansion and growth the Second. Why this difference?

To this there is no easy answer. Economics is a field of knowledge in which, unfortunately, conflicting interpretations can all be made to appear more or less plausible. Mathematical

[1] These concepts were coined by Henry C. Wallich in his *Mainsprings of the German Revival,* Yale University Press, 1955.

I

proof is not possible. Conclusions reached finally rest very much on one's set of values, and, to make matters worse, not infrequently, in the history of economic thought, the more incredible the theory the greater its fascination. There are examples of this both with respect to the interwar period and with respect to recent events. A careful screening of the economic literation of the last forty years or so, from this point of view, would be rewarding.

My own interpretation and analysis of the events following the two world wars will in all probability prove to be convincing to some of my readers and unconvincing to others. To this I am accustomed. The experience of the last twenty years shows clearly, however, that controversy is of high educational value. Economic thinking, both on the part of professional economists and on the part of the public generally, has undergone in recent years a very substantial change.

The change in thinking reflects the changes in economic life. After the First World War the efforts at adaptation to new conditions were largely unsuccessful; the result was, broadly speaking, world-wide economic stagnation. After the Second World War the economic policies adopted proved to be far more successful; the result was an almost incredible outburst of economic progress.

Germany and the United Kingdom best exemplify the general world plight throughout most of the interwar period. In the United Kingdom unemployment averaged 14.2 per cent for eighteen long years from 1921 to 1938. Germany's record from the end of the astronomical inflation to Hitler's entrance on the stage was even worse—17.9 per cent for the ten years 1923 to 1932, inclusive.[2] In the United States following the

---

[2] See Ingvar Svennilson, *Growth and Stagnation in the European Economy*, United Nations Economic Commission for Europe, Geneva, 1954. German employment increased greatly after 1933, but the figures are not available.

boom twenties average unemployment for the twelve-year period 1930 to 1941, inclusive, was 17.2 per cent.

With this vast amount of unemployment it is not surprising that real income in Western Europe, in the interwar period (despite some considerable increases in *man-hour* productivity) was only slightly higher than prewar. In the United Kingdom the per capita real income in the twelve years 1921 to 1932, inclusive, *averaged* 2 per cent below 1913—far short of the normal growth trend. At the end of the thirties the United Kingdom experienced a considerable recovery, but by 1938 per capita real income was still only 20 per cent above the level reached a quarter of a century before. In Germany (omitting the disastrous years of astronomical inflation) per capita real income averaged 12 per cent below 1913 in the twelve years from 1925 to 1936, inclusive. For France the average for 1921 to 1938 was indeed 11.7 per cent above 1913 —a much better record, yet far below the level that could normally be expected. In the United States, averaging the entire eighteen years from 1921 to 1938, per capita real income was only 14.7 per cent above prewar—far below the growth trend.[3] The United States (and to a degree also France) did well in the twenties but performed disastrously in the thirties. The United Kingdom and Germany, on the other hand, performed badly in the twenties and in the early thirties, but both had short recoveries in the later thirties.

Taking a simple average of all four countries, per capita real income for the entire interwar period stood only 5 per cent above prewar. At the end of the interwar period (i.e., the peak of the postwar boom, so called) the per capita real income was only 18 per cent above that of 1913. And it took just twenty years after the war to reach this level.

In contrast, the record after the Second World War is indeed a miracle of performance. After only nine years the

[3] *Ibid.*, p. 233.

average *per capita* income of the three big European countries was 23 per cent above prewar. For the United States the gain was 67 per cent. *Industrial* production per capita increased somewhat more rapidly than per capita real income. For the three large European countries the average per capita increase of industrial output was 26 per cent and for the United States 80 per cent above prewar.

Calculated on a per annum basis, the progress after the Second World War was three times as great for the three large European countries as after the First World War. For the United States the increase in output per annum was seven times as great as in the interwar period.

Unemployment following the Second World War was reduced to a level that had generally come to be regarded as impossible of attainment without creating violent inflation. In the United States unemployment averaged only 3.8 per cent from 1946 to 1955, and for some months it fell to 2.0 per cent. In the United Kingdom the figure has hovered around 1.5 per cent, at times almost reaching the vanishing point. In Germany the employment record is far from being as good as it might be but is immeasurably better than in the interwar period. After the inflation following the First World War, the average unemployment for ten years was 17.9 per cent of the labor force. In the recent five-year period from 1950 to 1954 the average was 7.6 per cent.

Associated with the high level of employment and production in the Western world following the Second World War is an extraordinarily high volume of investment. Among the European countries, Norway leads the way with investment constituting 29 per cent [4] of Gross National Product (GNP). Then come Holland and Germany with 24 and 23 per cent,

[4] For these calculations I have used the average for the years 1950, 1952, and 1954. See *Economic Survey of Europe in 1955*, United Nations, Geneva, 1956.

Sweden with 20 per cent, the United States with 17–18 per cent, and the United Kingdom with 13 per cent. Investment in the United Kingdom has indeed been far too low but nonetheless distinctly superior to the record following the First World War.

B. Depressing Factors in the Interwar Period

With respect to the poor showing following the First World War two things can, it seems to me, be said. The first is this: Powerful forces were at work tending to produce a condition of prolonged stagnation. The second is the fact that governments all over the Western world were bewildered, unprepared to assume responsibility for maximizing output and employment, unresourceful in meeting new conditions, relying instead upon outmoded policies—policies that were reasonably adequate for nineteenth-century conditions but not suitable for the problems of the interwar period. Had we known then what we now do, we should never have allowed the stagnation, the vast unemployment, and the loss of real income which actually was experienced by the Western world in the interwar decades.

The First World War constitutes a great divide. At this point in history the Western world somehow shifted from buoyant optimism to bleak pessimism. This shift was, however, not merely psychological. It was due to real factors. Psychology, in economic affairs, is not an ultimate cause. It is a medium of transmission. Real factors account basically for the shift in expectations. These factors lie deeper than the war itself. And Western Europe was not prepared to meet the change.

The pre-1914 economy had experienced a rapid growth in population, and along with this a high rate of capital accumulation. Employment ran on a high level, and there was a rapid increase in productivity. Against the pessimistic view of some early nineteenth-century writers, there developed, under Alfred Marshall's leadership, a picture of continued progress, broken only by brief lapses from full employment.

From 1880 to 1914 the output of European manufacturing industry increased by 3¼ per cent per year. Cost-reducing investment was rapidly raising man-hour productivity. Capital formation was proceeding apace, not only to implement new techniques but also to provide the capital goods needed by reason of the rapid increase in population. "It can be expected," says Professor Ingvar Svennilson, "that the extent to which industries expand or stagnate will depend on the rate at which the population is increasing. When population is increasing rapidly, most industries will expand." [5] Thus both technologically inspired autonomous investment and also "derived demand," or induced investment, were running high in the pre-1914 period. Accordingly the average *age* of capital equipment was low. Half of the capital stock of Western Europe had been built within the previous ten years.

From these *real* factors a buoyant psychology developed. There was a widespread belief in continued expansion. A buoyant optimism set the stage for new and expanding enterprises. "It is difficult to appreciate fully the effects of this long period of expansion upon the psychology of the European economy." [6]

This period of long-term progress came to an end. The war is often cited as a cause. But so far as the war itself is concerned, it could equally have set off a new period of expansion, as has happened both before and since. In view of this historic fact, the war is obviously not a satisfactory explanation for the stagnation which followed. The checks to long-term

[5] Ingvar Svennilson, *op. cit.*, p. 10.
[6] *Ibid.*, p. 18.

growth lie deeper. The cessation of long-term growth is due
to a "complicated cumulative process." [7]

Says Svennilson: "The slowing-down of the rate of increase
of population after the First World War in some of the more
developed European countries may . . . afford one explanation of why the employment level in these countries fell so
low, and not only during periods of depression." [8]

Taylorism and the so-called rationalization movement,
being capital-saving developments, started the downturn in the
ratio of capital to output which has characterized the last three
decades. This in itself was a good thing, assuming that the
ratio of consumption to income could have been raised. But
given the propensity to consume, investment was too low to
maintain full employment, too low to permit the warranted
rate of growth. Thus there developed the new phenomenon
of underemployment equilibrium. Unemployment was no
longer a function merely of cyclical depression. Secular unemployment was now piled on top of cyclical unemployment.

Investment was, moreover, affected by the rising overseas
competition from the new industries rapidly growing up in
the hitherto-underdeveloped countries. The prewar overseas
outlet for investment suffered a severe setback. European business circles continued far into the twenties to expect a return
to prewar normalcy. They could not believe that the old lush
days were over. With their eyes riveted by force of habit on
overseas investment, it required more than a decade of hard
times to convince them that they had better cultivate their
own gardens. They did not understand that changed conditions demanded a shift from extensive expansion to intensive
expansion. Not until the late thirties did they seriously begin
to turn inward to internal, domestic investment.

[7] *Ibid.*, p. 19.
[8] *Ibid.*, p. 11.

Economic policies failed to match up with the changed conditions. Emphasis continued to be placed on classical lines of policy. Cost-price theory dominated, not the theory of aggregate demand, growth, and employment. Remedies were sought in a return to the gold standard, in fixed exchanges, in wage cuts. The result was a "policy of deflation with widespread unemployment." [9] This policy of deflation was highly unfavorable to a rapid transformation of industry. The emphasis placed on international finance and trade distracted attention from the main task at hand, namely, home investment, employment, living standards, and, in general, the goals of the welfare state.

Foreign trade and autonomous investment were too meager to generate full employment. Accordingly the levels of income and output were too low, the periods of prosperity too short and too anemic to permit any strong acceleration effect from "derived demand." New developments were not afforded sufficient time to germinate. Aggregate demand was never sufficient to generate growth and expansion.

Thus mass unemployment appeared even in periods of so-called prosperity. Concealed and submerged unemployment had indeed long been a familiar phenomenon in capital-poor, underdeveloped countries where labor lacked the necessary complementary factors of production. But in capital-rich, industrially developed countries, long-term unemployment had, on classical lines of thinking, been regarded as an impossibility. Now, in the interwar period, underemployment became a deeply ingrained element in the economic system. English economists spoke at first almost incredulously about the "third winter of unemployment." As time wore on, year after year for nearly two decades, they came to accept as more or less inevitable the continued hard core of unemployment. What

[9] *Ibid.*, p. 24.

was needed was a new orientation, a new outlook, new goals, and new policies to convert a low-employment economy into a high-employment economy.

Deflation was the traditional remedy. Deflation was supposed to "cleanse the system," to eliminate weak firms, to increase the efficiency of labor. Instead, the experience of the interwar years indicated that the deflation often failed to eliminate weak firms, which continued to cling on desperately, clogging the market with excess capacity. Deflation, instead of bringing about reorganization with strengthened equity capital, tended to burden companies with top-heavy debt and hindered the process of modernization. Labor, instead of being driven out of low-wage, obsolete industries, became highly immobile in an oversaturated market.

In the generally stagnant interwar years three countries did indeed, for special reasons, prosper in the twenties, namely, France, Sweden, and the United States. In France per capita real income by 1929 was 32 per cent above prewar, in Sweden 33 per cent, and in the United States 38 per cent. But France and the United States suffered a dreadful retreat throughout most of the thirties, leaving their aggregate interwar record of per capita real income only 11.4 per cent and 14.7 per cent above prewar. The depression of the thirties, both in France and in the United States, constituted a severe offset to the prosperity of the twenties. Moreover, averages obscure the fact that unemployment and bankruptcy are always concentrated on a fraction of the population. For the millions of totally unemployed the figure for average employment is no comfort.

Sweden alone continued to move forward to substantially higher real income per capita throughout the entire interwar period. Thus her per capita real income was 33 per cent above prewar by 1929 and 70 per cent above prewar by 1938.

C. Transition to High-Pressure Economics

For Western Europe as a whole and for the United States, the interwar period was one of transition. It was a transition from nineteenth-century economic liberalism to those forms of national economic planning involved in the emergence of the welfare state. It was not (except to a very limited degree in England and France) a movement away from private enterprise. Private enterprise is stronger, more buoyant, more dynamic today in all Western Europe and also in the United States than it was in the interwar period. It was not a transition from private to public ownership. It was a transition from an individualistic economy to a mixed public-private economy with emphasis on social welfare.

Increasingly there was emerging the growing political influence of the working classes. They were demanding redistribution of income, progressive taxation, social security—in short, the welfare state. The emergence of national policies often involved temporary use of controls, import controls, price controls, subsidies for agriculture, and subsidies for housing. The market economy was, however, not discarded; yet it was indeed given less free play. It came to be realized that often, as in the case of agricultural surpluses in the United States, a free market had little effect in the desired direction. People were becoming aware that serious distortions in underlying supply-and-demand conditions—distortions often arising from the war—could only lead to violent maladjustments in the price structure if the market were given free rein. State intervention was utilized in England to reduce excess capacity in textiles and to infuse new energy in steel. Slowly it began to be recognized that, here and there at least, state intervention could be "decisive in speeding up the process of transformation." [10]

[10] *Ibid.*, p. 37.

The transition involved increasing emphasis on stability. Stability of income and employment became a goal with a "value in its own right." Critics advanced the thesis that the slowing-down of progress in the interwar years was itself a result of this growing emphasis on stability. [11] But as we moved into the forties and fifties it became increasingly apparent that this was not a necessary consequence. We have at long last learned that it is possible to have both stability and progress. Greater equality of income distribution is not incompatible with high ratios of investment to Gross National Product.

The transition did indeed usher in a leveling-down of the very large incomes. Low incomes were raised and supplemented by old-age pensions and other social-security benefits. Dividend policy became more restrictive; interest rates were lowered. "The share of the national income held by the very rich was definitely crumbling," [12] at least in much of Western Europe. But capital formation nevertheless went on apace. Internal financing, pension and insurance funds, and streams of social saving were supplanting the capital market and the individual savings of the rich. In these latter days we have learned, beyond peradventure of a doubt, that it does not require nineteenth-century high concentration of income or sole reliance on personal saving to ensure a completely adequate volume of capital formation.

This transition has shifted Western Europe and the United States from a low-employment, stagnant economy to a high-employment, buoyant, and dynamic economy. It has transferred the Western world from low-pressure economics to high-pressure economics.

It could, of course, be argued, not without reason, that the high-pressure, full-employment economics experienced after

[11] *Ibid.*, p. 38.
[12] *Ibid.*, p. 40.

the Second World War is purely an accident and has nothing to do with policy. This is indeed true in no inconsiderable measure. This undeniable fact is, however, likely to obscure something that is very real, namely, the basic and fundamental change that has occurred in the outlook and purpose of countries in the Western world. It is true that the cold war, Marshall Plan aid, Korea, the spreading of the conflict into new areas in the Far East, the Middle East, and Africa, have forced on the entire Western world vastly enlarged public budgets which have tended to place the economy under pressure. But it is also true that, had the old climate of opinion continued to prevail, this very fact would have indicated a policy of rigorous retrenchment in other directions—the policy indeed of low-pressure economics.

D. Low-Pressure Economics in Germany

This, in fact, is precisely what has occurred in one of the leading countries of Western Europe, namely, Germany. This development has led to a pseudo revival of economic liberalism (using that phrase in its French meaning) and has revitalized the advocacy of a number of policies stemming from the old pre-1914 laissez-faire tradition.

Germany has indeed in some measure practiced, since the currency reform of 1948, a policy of low-pressure economics, low wages, curtailment of consumption, and a considerable margin of unemployment.

This policy, it is true, made possible an earlier ending of rationing and price control than had been possible in most other European countries. It is, however, not true that Germany can be cited as a perfect example of economic liberalism, namely, a competitive society operating in a truly free-price market. Germany historically is par excellence the country of cartels, and while the American Military Government made some effort to weaken the hold of cartels, the effort has met with relatively little success, and such success as there was appears to be rapidly vanishing. Germany, moreover, has a long tradition as a paternalistic and authoritarian government with respect to economic affairs. This continues to play a role in innumerable ways. Only a country with this tradition could, for example, have introduced the famous Investment Assistance Plan, by which contributions were assessed upon all large industrial firms. These assessments were in effect collected like a tax but were really a form of compulsory investment forced by law upon consumer-goods industries and the lighter industries in order to supply funds to the so-called bottleneck industries, namely, iron and steel, coal, and public utilities.

The tradition of paternalism and authoritarianism in government is, moreover, well illustrated in the tax-incentive schemes instituted in the postwar period. These involved, among other things, tax exemption, up to stipulated amounts, for income saved or invested in designated ways. These tax exemptions applied to such things as life-insurance premiums and other forms of savings, and to funds loaned for house construction. A part of business income was tax-exempt if retained and invested in the business or used for repairs and reconstruction. Businesses, at the time of the monetary reform in 1948, were permitted to revalue their assets more or less arbitrarily. This led to large annual write-offs, thereby reducing current taxes and facilitating the flowing-back of earnings into investment. The Germans, while talking abstractly about economic liberalism, have, in fact, always been ingenious at implementing forms of state intervention.

Germany has, moreover, a long tradition of government ownership and operation of enterprises. While theorizing a great deal about the virtues of free and private enterprise, Germany is even today par excellence the country that most conspicuously exemplifies a highly developed *state* capitalism. This is, of course, a matter of long standing, going back in part even to the days of Bismarck. The Government owns and operates the railroads. There are a not-inconsiderable number of industrial enterprises owned and operated by the Government, including the famous automobile concern the Volkswagen. There are a number of mixed public-private enterprises. Public utilities, the radio, the telegraph, telephone, local transportation systems, municipal savings banks, etc., are publicly owned. There is surely a wide chasm between the ideals of nineteenth-century economic liberalism and the far-flung role of the Government in the German economy.

Germany is, moreover, by no means a laggard with respect to the development of the welfare state. Here, also, beginnings can be traced back to Bismarck. In addition to old-age, invalidity, and unemployment insurance, there is a compulsory system of public-health insurance (nationalized medicine) which in the United States is usually regarded as the most advanced exhibit of the welfare state and sometimes referred to as "creeping" and sometimes as "galloping" socialism.

Nor is Germany behind most other countries with respect to the size of the public budgets (about 35 per cent) in relation to the national income. And with respect to the role of *government* in capital formation, Germany is clearly outstanding. It is said that one-fourth of total investment is made by government—federal, state, or local. In addition to the Reconstruction Loan Corporation, one may note the large investments in government enterprises, in public utilities of all kinds, and also the role played by government with respect to housing. This takes various forms, including subsidies made partly in the form of capital sums and partly in low-interest loans with long periods of amortization. Housing is, of course, an area in which the government plays a leading role in all modern countries, including even the United States, but

Germany is well out in front. Present-day Germany is thus scarcely an example of simon-pure free enterprise or nine-teenth-century liberalism.

It is, however, true, as already indicated, that Germany freed herself decisively, after the monetary reform of June, 1948, from rationing and price controls. In this respect, in contrast with most other European countries, particularly the United Kingdom, the Scandinavian countries, and Holland, it is perfectly legitimate to refer to her economy as a "free-market" or "free-enterprise" economy.

In pursuit of her free-market policy, it became necessary to ease the pressure for consumers' goods. In contrast with the high aggregate demand in Britain and the Scandinavian coun-tries (consumption, investment, and government postwar re-quirements all competing urgently for the limited supplies), Germany pursued a policy of *suppressed* consumption in order to make room for a large volume of investment and in addition to provide sufficient slack so that there would be no upward pressure on prices in a free market. Wages were held down, and unemployment on a considerable scale was justified as necessary in order to prevent inflationary pressures. Unem-ployment averaged 10 per cent of the labor force in 1950, 8.3 per cent in 1951, and 6.6 per cent in 1952–1954. The flood of refugees from the east helped to keep wages down. German trade-unionism had gone through a disillusioning experience under Hitler and the war, and had become largely incapable of pressing vigorously the demands of labor.

Income distribution shifted heavily toward the rich. While in 1913 and again in 1938 the lower half of the population re-ceived 23 to 24 per cent of total income, by 1950 it received only 16 per cent. In contrast, the top 5 per cent received 27 per cent. The degree of concentration which this figure repre-sents will become more clearly evident when compared with that in the United States. While Germany's top 5 per cent

received 27 per cent of the total income, the American top
5 per cent received only 20 per cent.[13] While Germany's lower
half received only 16 per cent, in the United States it received
23 per cent. While Germany's income distribution has become
considerably more concentrated, in the United States we have
moved in the direction of less concentration. Tax policy, wage
policy, employment policy have operated to increase the wide
disparity of income between the rich and the poor in Germany. The postwar Government in Germany has been a businessman's government.

Germany's low-pressure economic policy has nonetheless
not resulted in disastrously high unemployment. Indeed unemployment fell from 10 per cent in 1950 to 5.8 per cent in
1954 despite a large increase in the labor force. Aggregate
employment has been growing, and aggregate real income has
increased 60 per cent above prewar. Corrected for population
changes, including the 10 million refugees, this makes a per
capita gain in real income of 25 per cent above prewar. There
can be no question that Germany has experienced a remarkable recovery and can boast a very high record of achievement.

Impressed by this record, economists who are unfavorably
inclined toward economic planning, contend (a) that Germany's successful absorption of a growing labor force together
with her expanding productivity is due to her pursuit of low-
pressure economics and the early abandonment of rationing
and controls, and (b) that Germany's record shows the superiority of the policies pursued by Germany over those pursued by Britain, the Scandinavian countries, and Holland.

Is it true that low-pressure economic policy accounts for the
progress Germany has made? About this a number of things

[13] Henry C. Wallich, *Mainsprings of the German Revival*, Yale
University Press, 1955, p. 47; and National Bureau of Economic Research, Occasional Paper 35.

need to be said. First, it should be noted that there are very important real factors underlying the German recovery which would operate more or less regardless of the economic policy pursued. The German people are a physically vigorous and hard-working race. The labor force is technically competent, trained, and experienced. The entrepreneurs are alert, ingenious, inventive, highly educated as engineers, scientists, and business managers. German plant and equipment are modern and up to date. Even the destruction caused by the war had failed to knock out Germany's industrial capacity. The productive equipment constructed during the war probably exceeded the facilities destroyed during the war. It is estimated that at the end of the war Germany possessed slightly better than prewar industrial capacity.[14]

E. Germany in the Postwar World

A country which possesses a highly developed technique, a large stock of capital, an energetic entrepreneurial class, and an efficient labor force can accomplish wonders if it is given a reasonable chance. The postwar world (i.e., post-Second World War) gave Germany that chance. It is the outside world, into which Germany has been permitted to become integrated, which accounts in no small measure for the progress she has made. The success of her internal policy must be appraised in terms of the world background.

Germany's recovery was stagnating in 1949 and 1950 up to the time of Korea. The low-pressure economics was being weighed in the balance and found wanting. Under the pressure of growing unemployment a positive governmental program of expansion was somewhat reluctantly undertaken. Before it had gotten appreciably under way, the Korean boom struck. Germany's index of production jumped from 98 to 145 from

[14] Wallich, op. cit., p. 7.

the first quarter of 1950 to the second quarter of 1952, and the Gross National Product, in real terms, rose 50 per cent from 1949 to 1952. Under the stimulus of the Korean War and the rapidly expanding rearmament program, the world was clamoring for the products of German heavy industry. The outside world provided Germany with the stimulus of high-pressure economics which her own internal policy had denied her. Had there been no war, no rearmament, and no intensified cold war, and had the Western world itself generally pursued a policy of low-pressure economics, Germany's postwar record might have presented quite a different picture.

In the midst of this high level of world demand, with its induced effect on the internal German market, Germany pursued with a good deal of success the policy of low wages and restricted consumption, thereby making room for domestic investment and a high level of exports. Low wages relative to manufacturing prices had prevailed at the end of 1948. This spread had indeed nearly closed by the end of 1954, but man-hour productivity had also greatly increased in the meantime, affording still an abnormal basis for large profits. These profits were plowed back into industry. Germany's ratio of investment to GNP was high, and this was of the highest importance for a sound recovery.

F. The Social-Democratic Countries

But what about the social-democratic countries—the Scandinavian countries, Holland, and Great Britain—with their greater emphasis on consumption, with their high-pressure economics? Were they suffering from inadequate investment —inadequate in terms of the requirements of growth and expansion?

In general, the answer is No. Consumption was indeed given wider scope, but investment by and large has a record in those countries equal to and in some cases better than that of Germany. How could this be possible? The answer is that the policy of high-pressure economics gave these countries a fuller employment of the labor force. Norway's investment averaged 29.4 per cent of GNP for the three years 1950, 1952, and 1954, Holland's 23.6—both higher than the German figure of 23.1 per cent.[15] And while Sweden's ratio of investment to GNP was 3.5 percentage points below that of Germany, note should be made of the fact that Germany's postwar investment has consisted very heavily of inventory stocks. Fixed-capital investment is perhaps a more relevant figure, and here Sweden's record is very nearly the same as that of Germany—19.1 per cent compared with 20.3 per cent —despite the fact that Sweden had maintained an extraordinarily high rate of investment, almost without interruption, through the two interwar decades as well as in the more recent postwar years.

Thus the record does not disclose that Germany stands out ahead of the social-democratic countries with respect to this matter of investment. No conclusive argument can be made favoring low-pressure economics. It must of course be admitted that both England and France present an unsatisfactory record of capital accumulation, though better than in the interwar decades. This has become traditional with those countries, and the reasons are highly complex and difficult to unravel.

It is true that the policy of high-pressure economics pursued by the social-democratic countries compelled them to retain rationing and price controls for a prolonged period. Their people clearly preferred these hardships to unemployment, restricted consumption, and an undemocratic distribution of income. Yet, as the war-created scarcities of foodstuffs and

[15] *Economic Survey of Europe in 1955,* United Nations, Geneva, 1956.

other materials were gradually overcome, rationing and controls were abandoned. These countries have demonstrated that the oft-repeated assertion that controls once imposed can never be removed is not true. Democratic societies do not want controls for their own sake. Controls are accepted only when necessary.

Germany's Korean boom experience is itself a case in point. The outside stimulus pulled Germany up from a stagnating plateau to a level which her leaders had believed impossible. They had argued, against those who had advocated an expansionist program, that further advance in output and employment could not be achieved merely by increasing aggregate demand. The real trouble, so they thought, was structural, involving bottlenecks in certain key industries. But the Korean episode proved the contrary. Germany's economy responded to the outside stimulus. Employment and production increased sharply. This did, in fact, cause some increase in prices, and it created an international balance-of-payments crisis. To meet this situation, Germany was compelled to impose a number of rigid controls, contrary to her free-market principles. But the country was happy with the outcome. The growth in employment and real income was worth the price.

G. Problems Confronting High-Pressure Economics

Low-pressure economics does indeed simplify the problem of price stability and also the balance-of-payments problem. A full-employment, high-pressure economy has its problems. But advanced democratic countries are committed to full employment. They demand the highest standard of living which an advancing economy can provide. They demand both high investment and high consumption. They demand a high level of capital formation, and yet they desire a more equitable distribution of income. To these seemingly contradictory demands the older economics offered no solution. But in the modern advanced democracies easy negative answers are not tolerated. The circle has to be squared. We are compelled to find a way to achieve full employment together with both growth and stability, yet without freezing the system under the weight of intolerable controls. The result is solutions that are neither white nor black but nonetheless workable.

Experience in recent years, both in Western Europe and in the United States, offers a good deal of encouragement. In the United States, no one will deny that throughout most of the period since the end of the Second World War our economy has been operating under high pressure, yet with a minimum of controls. Once the controls were removed in mid 1946, it is true that prices rose under the impact of the terrific backlog of demand and the prevailing shortages. But the moderate inflation that ensued (to the astonishment of many, if not most, economists) quickly petered out within eighteen months. And for two and a half years before Korea wholesale prices trended gently downward. It is true that for eight months the Korean buying spree again caused a price spurt, but this also quickly vanished. For six years we have had fairly stable prices with unemployment averaging not much above 3 per cent. Since January, 1948, we have experienced a degree of price stability, despite the Korean bulge, rarely matched in our entire history. Collective bargaining and full-employment policies do not appear to be as dangerously inflationary as had been supposed. We are certainly not out of the woods and we need to remain alert. But I note with a good deal of satisfaction that the inflation alarmists are beating the drums a good deal less vigorously than was the case a few years ago.

Formerly price stability or instability was left largely to the play of automatic forces. Apart from wartime, the record was indeed reasonably good. Today we are very conscious, and rightly so, of the problem. We are conscious of it because we now have a *managed* economy. We cannot leave it to chance. Up to date I think it is fair to say that we have acted pretty responsibly. We have had no wild inflation. It is just not true that we have been living in a period of continuous inflation. Since the end of the war we have had some 30 months of inflationary price rises and 105 months of substantial price stability. The inflationary periods were directly caused by war—the first by the overwhelming shortages created by the Second World War and the second by the Korean crisis. Apart from the war episodes, we have experienced a degree of stability which has, I believe, surprised nearly everyone. We have had responsible fiscal and monetary policies, and we have had responsible collective bargaining. If war comes again, then of course all bets are off. But if we can have peace, the evidence to date is that as a people we take very seriously the responsible task of managing a high-pressure economy. And I do not believe that we are prepared to ease the task of responsible management at the price of less than full employment.

The American Economy works best under pressure. It was high-pressure economics which called forth the more than $100 billion increase in output of goods and services (measured in dollars of constant value) from 1946 to 1956. Our prodigious capacity to increase output when demand expands, the wide margin of savings generated by high income levels, and our demonstrated willingness to impose necessary taxes represent powerful safeguards against inflation. The United States is not an inflation-sensitive country.

The social-democratic countries are confronted with somewhat more difficult problems, but they are all seasoned societies with a high sense of political and social responsibility. They do not act capriciously. Measured against the three classical criteria of a well-functioning economy, namely, a high value of capital formation, rising productivity, and a reasonably equitable distribution of income, they have all performed amazingly well. They have demonstrated their desire to do away as fast as possible with unnecessary controls. They prefer a free market. They are committed to the welfare state, but there is no urge to nationalize industry. They continue to face balance-of-payments problems. The solution for this is not clear. There is greater freedom of exchange now than some years ago, and we have by now almost reached, in fact, convertibility. Perhaps we shall never achieve complete convertibility. Perhaps here, as elsewhere, the answer may not be either all white or all black. We have already moved toward a mixed solution, more freedom but not complete freedom. In the meantime we are doing very well. In no event shall we sell full employment "down the river" in exchange for so small a token as perfect convertibility. Convertibility looms large in restricted financial circles, but in the modern world more important values are to be found in full employment and rising living standards.

The answer to stagnation is not the dogma of automatic adjustment. The answer is the vastly enlarged role of democratic governments—the assumption of responsibility for the maintenance of full employment.

CHAPTER 2

THE AMERICAN ECONOMY
ON THE MARCH

A. A Full-Employment Economy

The American Economy has undergone a considerable re-modeling during the last quarter-century. I begin with what I regard as by far the most important single factor. It is a new factor, never before experienced in American history. And it is this. We have not had a major depression since 1938. Nearly two decades without a serious downturn. We had, indeed, a minor dip in 1949 and again in 1954—light jolts but no serious depression. And we have had virtually continuous full employment since 1941, a period of fifteen years. Now this is something distinctly new, and we would do well to take a good look at this strange and quite novel experience.

I repeat, we have had virtually full employment and booming prosperity for sixteen years. Past experience has been quite different. Throughout our history every eight or nine years we have experienced serious depression and widespread unemployment. Indeed our economy was for a hundred years the most violently fluctuating economy in the world. And in the 1930s we had prolonged depression and seemingly endless stagnation.

Why has our experience since the Second World War been so different from that of earlier decades? To this there are two answers, and one of them unhappily involves *war* and the dark clouds of international relations. The second answer, however, carries with it at least the possibility of *peaceful* growth, full employment, and expansion.

First let us consider the military factor. At the end of the thirties the United States was possessed of a highly efficient stock of productive equipment. During the great depression there developed indeed large excess capacity in view of the depressed market, and net additions to plant and equipment were pretty meager. Nevertheless, replacement and modernization were going on. The aggregate value of replacement and modernization of plant, equipment, houses, and fixed capital in general for the entire decade 1931 to 1940 (in terms of 1955 prices) amounted to the by no means insignificant sum of $165 billion. The American Economy, when it began to function in 1941 as the arsenal of democracy, was already an industrial giant equipped with modern techniques, large excess capacity, ingenious and daring entrepreneurs, and a labor force with a long background experience in industrial techniques. This industrial giant was raring to go. It had not had a chance to show what it could do for an entire decade. The lull had, however, not brought deterioration. The American giant, though it had been forced to curtail operations, had refurbished its tools. It was prepared to go forward. The American Economy had acquired already by 1941 an immense potential capacity. All that it needed was an adequate market for its products.

This market the war supplied. Four hundred and fifty billions of dollars (in 1955 prices) were spent on war matériel and military outlays in the five years 1941 to 1945. Yet despite this vast expenditure of productive resources on war and national security, $100 billion were spent in the aggregate in these five years on private domestic investment in capital goods of all kinds, only $17 billion less than in the preceding five peaceful years and $50 billion more than in the five deep depression years of 1931 to 1935—all figures being in terms of 1955 prices. But it is in the area of consumption that a real miracle occurred. Besides producing $450 billion of war material and $100 billion of plant, machinery, and other capital goods, we produced in the five war years $790 billion of consumers' goods (1955 prices), or $125 billion more than in the prewar five-year period.[1] The war put the American giant to work, and once fully employed, we found that we were able to raise our standard of living by a considerable margin beyond any level previously achieved at the very time we were fighting a total war. This no one would have believed until it actually happened.

The lesson to learn is this: Efficiency, adequate plant and equipment, able entrepreneurs, and skilled workmen are not enough. These alone do not give us prosperity or full employment. The one thing missing before the war, the one thing the American Economy needed, was adequate *aggregate demand*.

During the war years aggregate personal income far exceeded the output of civilian goods. The American people set aside out of this excess income a large amount of savings. Pent-up demands accumulated. Until these were worked off, there was little danger of a recurrence of inadequate demand. At the end of the war, consumer stocks of durables and semi-durables and business stocks of inventories had to be replenished.

Yet it soon became evident that the end of the war had not brought the peace. The international clouds gathered again. National-security expenditures averaged $22 billion per year (1955 prices) in the first five postwar years. Then came Korea, and in the next five years, 1951 to 1955, military and security

[1] This statement needs to be qualified as follows: (*a*) Some goods were unavailable, (*b*) some available goods were of a poorer quality, and (*c*) population had increased.

expenditures rose to an average of $46 billion per year. This included the Korean war expenditures as well as the general build-up of our military plant and equipment. After hostilities ceased, national-security expenditures [2] declined, but they still amounted to $41 billion in the calendar year 1955.

In view of these vast expenditures it is not difficult to see why we have had full employment. The American Economy has been operating under pressure. First the war, then the pent-up demands, then Korea, and then the cold war. Under pressure the economy has responded magnificently. In the first half of the postwar decade, $200 billion consumers' goods were produced per annum—$67 billion per annum in excess of the five prewar years. And during the last five years, 1951 to 1955, the annual output of consumers' goods amounted to $233 billion, or $100 billion per annum in excess of the five prewar years. All figures are in terms of 1955 prices.

Nor did private investment in capital goods suffer. In the first five postwar years, aggregate investment outlays amounted to $46 billion per annum, or nearly double the five prewar years. And during the last five years, average aggregate investment amounted annually to $55 billion, or $31 billion per annum in excess of the five prewar years. All together we have spent on *producers'* plant and equipment alone $300 billion since the end of the Second World War. The postwar gaps in our productive capacity were quickly filled. Particularly in our heavy-goods industries, capacity has been expanded to meet the military demands together with the requirements of growth and expansion in our civilian industries.

Sometimes we hear politicians suggest that our country is on

[2] This includes all national-defense expenditures for goods and services (including civil defense) but not such items relating to past wars as outlays for veterans or for the payment of interest on the national debt.

the verge of bankruptcy. Nothing could be further from the truth. Our military expenditures have not made us poor. They have put us to work. And full employment has given American business an unprecedented market for consumers' goods and capital goods alike. Never before have we been so well equipped with producers' capital or with consumer durables despite fifteen years of unprecedented outlays on the destructive weapons of war. This is indeed the paradox of the modern economy. Put to the test, the American Economy has evidenced a miraculous power to produce.

This is one side of the picture, and no amount of political semantics can change this fact. But this is not the whole picture. Were this all that could be said, there would indeed be ground for pessimism. Must we forever look forward to a world in which only vast military expenditures can assure us continuous full employment? That depends upon what we choose to do. The experience of the last decade is at least hopeful. We have been developing a new partnership between government and private enterprise. We have been learning a good deal about how to manage the economy.

B. Government's Contribution to the Reconversion Process

Not infrequently one hears it said that the postwar experience reveals "what the economy can do on its own," altogether apart from any role the government may play. This view overlooks, however, the postwar government budgets and the backlog of demand caused by the war. Anyone is entitled to his own *convictions* about what the economy might or might not have been able to do on its own. But no one can truthfully say that the postwar upsurge has demonstrated what the economy, unaided by government, can do on its own. Quite the contrary. One is impressed with the enormous amount of fuel that is required to keep the American productive giant fully employed.

The speed of the conversion from war to peace has sometimes been credited to the free operations of the private-enterprise economy. Now this is indeed in no small measure true. Industry proved to be flexible and adjustable, and the labor force, swollen during the war by from 7 to 8 million emergency workers, quickly fell back to peacetime levels. But it is also well to remember that the thing didn't "just happen." Government did play an important role in the adjustment process immediately following the war. There were the veterans' terminal-leave benefits; the gigantic veterans' training program, involving 8 million veterans at a cost of $1,800 per veteran; aid to disabled veterans; veterans' life insurance; and some $21 billion of loans for veterans' purchase of homes, farms, and businesses. There were, moreover, the various Acts passed by Congress to aid business in the reconversion process, the Contract-Settlement Act, for example. Already by the end of 1945 over 300,000 war contracts had been terminated, involving a commitment value of $63.5 billion. These settlements, typically generous to business, aided in the rapid reconversion of industry from war to peace.

There was, moreover, the Surplus Property Act, under which plants built by the government were disposed of to private businesses in order to promote a speedy recovery. Plants were often sold at 20 cents on the dollar.[3] The war-built manufacturing facilities alone amounted to well over one-half of the value of all manufacturing plants in existence in 1940.[4]

There was the repeal of the excess-profits tax immediately after the war despite the fact that large excess profits continued

[3] See statement by Senator O'Mahoney in Aaron Director (ed.), *Defense, Controls, and Inflation*, University of Chicago Press, 1952, p. 234.

[4] *America's Needs and Resources*, Twentieth Century Fund, 1955.

to be made long after the end of hostilities. Since these profits were due to the vast war-created shortages, they, in fact, were war profits. The Revenue Acts provided for a carry-back of unused excess profits credits and a carry-back of business losses. There was, moreover, provided a postwar refund of 10 per cent of the excess-profits tax payable soon after the end of the war. And the government had been sufficiently generous in the war contracts to permit large corporate profits after taxes, leaving the corporations in a very strong financial position at the close of the war.

The point to note is that it cannot truthfully be said that the government played no major role in the reconversion process. There was positive governmental intervention. The economy did not just operate on its own during the reconversion years.

C. Remodeling the American Economy

Following the reconversion process we have met successfully two mild and short recessions, either one of which might have developed into a serious depression. That they did not do so was not altogether a mere accident. The great depression, beginning with the 1929 crash, disclosed a number of serious weaknesses in the structure of the American Economy. Here and there the foundation crumbled, and this contributed to the collapse. This was true of the banking structure, of the capital and real-estate markets, and of our perverted fiscal procedures and practices.

The great depression made it crystal-clear that our economic structure, built on nineteenth-century laissez-faire principles and adapted to a rural, individualistic society, was hopelessly out of date. The nineteenth-century economy leaped forward with terrific strides but with violent fluctuations. These fluctuations fed upon themselves. Once started they cumulated. The system had no brakes either in its dizzy upward flights or in its devastating downspins. Instead, there was built into this system an accelerating mechanism which, reinforced by waves of pessimism and optimism, gave us highly speculative booms and deep depressions. Yet up to the First World War it was indeed true that powerful growth factors always lifted the economy back on the path of expansion. There was the vast pulling suction of the great West and the upsurge of population growth, two and one-half times as great, in relation to Gross National Product, as the current upsurge of population. Technological developments (a more constant factor) also helped to create a buoyant climate. But as we left the nineteenth century behind, the forces making for *extensive* expansion began to decline. Technology alone retained its undiminished vigor.

The stagnation of the thirties forced us to undertake a remodeling of our economic system. We have equipped the economic machine with cushions which tend to stop the headlong crash into deep depression. The consumption base has been broadened and made stronger. Not only has the consumption base been widened, it has also been isolated in some measure from income fluctuations. The *extensive* forces having weakened, we have done a good deal to strengthen the forces making for *intensive* expansion.

This result has been accomplished by means of the so-called built-in stabilizers and by other reforms. The built-in stabilizers act to sustain spendable incomes (i.e., incomes after taxes). They do this by causing tax revenues to fluctuate more than income and by counterfluctuations in transfer payments. The social-security programs, collective bargaining, the progressive income tax, the farm programs, guarantee of bank deposits, lending and insuring operations of the government, the housing programs, reforms in the mortgage and capital markets— all these help to sustain income.

We have, moreover, greatly strengthened the financial reserves of individuals, and this increases their buying power when unemployment begins to spread. The liquid wealth held by the private sector of the economy has greatly increased during the last twenty-five or thirty years. The accumulated savings of individuals and families, after correcting for price changes, have increased from $75 billion in 1925 to $175 billion in 1955. Thirty years ago only 45 per cent of urban homes were owned by the occupant. Today it is 57 per cent. Farm ownership has increased from 58 per cent to 75 per cent. The widespread holdings of United States savings bonds and the growth of life insurance and savings deposits, and of pension funds, provide the American Economy with an unparalleled accumulation of liquid assets which act as cushions against any serious business recession.

A highly important ingredient in our postwar prosperity has been the high level of housing construction. This, again, is no accident. Today housing rests largely on government programs. Over two-fifths of the entire home-mortgage debt is represented by loans insured or guaranteed by the Federal government.

D. The Public Debt

Sometimes we hear alarmists talk about our vast public debt. But rarely are we told about the powerful stabilizing role it plays in our economy. If every newspaper would publish on the front page every day a statement showing the ownership distribution of United States government securities, these alarmist statements would make little impression on the public mind. One-half of the public debt ($140 billion) is owned by the Federal Reserve banks, the commercial banks, and the Social Security Trust Funds. And of the remaining half, $100 billion is widely held by individuals in the form of savings bonds or by savings institutions, such as life insurance companies, savings banks, or pension funds, while $20 billion is held by corporations serving to strengthen the financial position and liquidity of business units. Only $15 billion is held by the upper-income group. The public debt is not owned by a few plutocrats to whom the mass of citizens pay tribute. The ownership of United States government securities is widely diffused over our entire savings and financial structure. The widespread ownership of the public debt, this vast reserve of liquid assets, constitutes a powerful line of defense against any serious recession.

Behind all this we have built up governmental machinery to deal actively with the problem of economic growth and stability. In the Employment Act of 1946, the Federal government assumed responsibility for the creation and maintenance of conditions under which the country could achieve maximum employment and production. This act was passed by an overwhelming bipartisan majority. It has been vigorously endorsed by President Eisenhower. Under the Act two responsible sentinels are created and placed on guard to warn the nation of danger signals. They are continuously at work planning programs of action when needed to stimulate expansion or to restrain an inflationary trend, as the case may be. One sentinel is planted in the Executive branch of the government—the President's Council of Economic Advisers; the other in the Congress—the Joint Committee on the Economic Report with its staff of economists. And they have not been idle. Tomes of hearings and reports have emerged, throwing a continuous spotlight on the economic scene and preparing the way for action when necessary.

E. Business Confidence Bolstered by Active Government Policy

The American Economy can no longer be described as a laissez-faire society where private enterprise is left to shift as best it can in the storms of a fluctuating and inadequate market.

No, our society has become a mixed public-private economy in which the powerful fiscal and monetary operations of an alert and informed government are playing a stabilizing and sustaining role. The announced readiness of the government to act, the continuing responsibility of the government to utilize all of its resources to promote stability and growth—this alone creates an atmosphere of confidence in the economic future of the country, a confidence which enables business to plan long-range investment programs and thus to contribute to the goal of sustained prosperity.

This leads me to comment briefly on a very interesting change in business sentiment. It was not many years ago that the steel companies were highly reluctant to increase their capacity. They looked back into their past, characterized by boom and bust. True, the Employment Act had been passed in 1946, but what assurance was there that full employment could be maintained? Would not the economy again experience violent fluctuations as it had throughout our history? In such a society it was only prudent to restrict investment in plant and equipment to a minimum. Barging ahead could only create excess capacity.

Over the years we have witnessed a considerable change in sentiment. Today, large-scale corporations are prepared to plan ahead. They have acquired a new confidence in the future. This confidence will be sadly misplaced if we do not succeed in maintaining steady growth at a rate something like 3 or 4 per cent per year. This is the challenge that confronts us. The new faith in the future has to be validated.

F. Sources of Investment Funds

Despite the heavy tax burden which the national-security program has imposed upon us, business has been able to find the necessary investment funds for the modernization and expansion of our growing industrial plant. Excluding partnerships and individual firms, business corporations have invested in the ten years 1946 to 1955, $200 billion in new plant and machinery. Where did all this money come from? During the first five postwar years, internal sources, namely, depreciation allowances and retained earnings, were large enough to finance this whole investment in plant and machinery. Other asset investments, including inventories and working capital, were covered by outside funds—bank loans and new issues. Of the total investment, two-thirds came from internal sources. During the last five years, 1951 to 1955, bank loans and new issues have increased slightly in importance. Still 64 per cent of total investment funds came from depreciation allowances and retained earnings—internal investment funds springing from within business corporations themselves.

Thus we have witnessed a laboratory experiment. This experiment discloses the fact that the price structure is capable of adjusting itself so that, despite an increase in corporate taxes from $1.4 billion in 1929 to $20.5 billion per annum in 1951 to 1955, the annual secretion, so to speak, of internal investment funds has tripled in this interval. Few people would have forecast this development had they been asked what would happen assuming an increase in corporate taxes such as we have in fact witnessed.

Sometimes one hears it said that with respect to external sources of funds a dangerous tendency has developed. During the last ten years, corporations have been able to raise funds by bond issues on much more favorable terms than by stock issues. This, it is said, has greatly increased bond financing. In the middle twenties the cost of new capital was about the same for both bond and stock issues—the bond-issue rate averaging 5.5 per cent for industrials, public utilities, and railroads, while the stock-issue rate (the dividend yield) was 5.7 per cent. In contrast, during the last ten years, 1946 to 1955, the cost of money through bond issues has been 3.2 per cent and on stock issues 5.2 per cent. Accordingly bond financing was cheaper. The striking fact is, however, that this favorable differential did not, in fact, result in a higher proportion of new bond issues relative to new stock issues. One might have supposed that corporations would surely be driven into bond issues and away from stock issues. Yet such has not been the case. During the last ten years the ratio of common-stock issues to total new issues has been almost exactly the same as in the middle twenties. In the years 1924 to 1926 only 26.9 per cent of total issues were stock issues, and during the last ten years it was 24 per cent—no significant change.

Clearly the factors determining decisions with respect to the stock-issue method of raising new capital versus the bond-issue method are very complex. The matter is clearly not decided purely in terms of sharpening pencils and figuring interest cost. Moreover, it should be noted that despite the traditional high ratio of new bond issues to stock issues, American industry is not thereby being weighed down with an increasing burden of debt. The reason is the fact already alluded to, namely, the vast amount of investment financed from retained earnings. Thus equity capital continues to grow despite the high ratio of bonds to stocks when new funds are sought in the capital market.

During the postwar period a very high investment program was needed to make good the war-created backlog of capital shortages and to implement fully the new techniques. Investment funds were urgently needed, and hence the great importance of high retained earnings. Dividends were deliberately kept down. Thus, while dividend payments increased only 67 per cent from 1929 to 1951–1955, profits after taxes increased 120 per cent.

During this catching-up process it is probable that the rate of capital investment to GNP has exceeded the long-term requirements of growth and expansion. If this be true, once this high investment ratio declines to a more normal level, a larger proportion of profits after taxes can and should be paid to stockholders in the form of dividends and to employees in higher wages.

We now come upon the thorny matter of venture capital. Apart from the increase in corporate taxes, what about the effect of the individual income tax upon the supply of venture capital? Have not the high upper-bracket rates cut off venture capital?

On balance the evidence is that this has not happened. A part of the explanation can be found in the low 25 per cent capital-gains tax. Combined with the high-bracket rates, the low capital-gains rate induces a flow of investment funds into new, growing, and dynamic industries.

Growth in capital facilities is well-nigh impossible in a poor, underdeveloped country. It can be achieved, however, with remarkable *speed* in a highly developed country which already has an advanced technique, a large stock of capital, and a capacity to produce far in excess of current consumption needs. "Our war-time experience demonstrated that deficiencies in the productive capacity of our physical plant can be quickly overcome." [5] During the decade of the forties our total manufacturing capacity increased 100 per cent.

G. *The Missing Link: Adequate Aggregate Demand*

What, then, is the essence of the American economic revolution of the last fifteen years? The miracle of production? The economy already had that *potential* back in the thirties, though the steam was unfortunately lacking. Now, however,

[5] *America's Needs and Resources,* Twentieth Century Fund, 1955, p. 940.

we have seen what the economy can do under the pressure of *adequate aggregate demand*. We now have acquired at least some confidence in the government's responsibility for the maintenance of prosperity and full employment. When the British Conservative Government, under Churchill, announced its assumption of continuing responsibility for high employment in 1944, that Act was regarded as a new venture of government, and so indeed it was. The Employment Act of 1946 set much the same goal for the United States. But it was not until President Eisenhower's statement with respect to the firm determination of his Administration to use the full powers of the government to prevent depression that general bipartisan acceptance of this program was achieved. It is indeed a revolution in men's thinking. And this revolution is in no small part the result of the vigorous economic controversies which have filled the pages of economic journals, and from there spilled out into the public forums, during the last two decades.

The American economic revolution involves not only a high-employment policy but also the introduction of the "welfare state." Indeed the welfare state constitutes a solid foundation upon which to build a full-employment program. It is the welfare state which has furnished us with most of the so-called "built-in stabilizers"—the progressive income tax, social-security payments, farm-support programs, etc. It is the welfare state which provides the continuing support of governmentally sponsored housing programs, rural electrification, and lending and guaranteeing operations. The welfare state is not socialism. Socialism is government ownership and operation of productive enterprise. We have seen no significant growth of public enterprise. In the recent Twentieth Century Fund volume we learn that employment in public enterprises in the United States, as a per cent of private employment, has increased only slightly, from 1.3 per cent in 1929 to 1.8 per cent in 1950. The welfare state does not consist of socialistic enterprises. The welfare state does, however, involve government outlays large enough [6] to permit fiscal policy to play a controlling role in the adjustment of aggregate demand to the productive potential of which the private-enterprise economy is capable. The government makes large expenditures, but private enterprise does the job. It is this that distinguishes the welfare state from socialism.

Now someone will say that the miracle of production which we have witnessed during the upsurge of the last fifteen years could never have occurred without the resourcefulness of private enterprise, the technical know-how, the technological innovations, and the capital formation necessary to implement the new technique. This is indeed unquestionably true, and it is a fact that should be stressed again and again. Yet even with respect to these factors it is important to note that the cause-and-effect relations are closely intertwined. The government has made a major contribution to ensure adequate aggregate demand. The upsurge related thereto has stimulated population growth, which in turn has contributed to the upsurge. The war and the postwar upsurge have served to stimulate new techniques, and these in turn reinforce the upsurge. And finally, investment in new capital (together with corporate and individual savings to finance it) is a consequence, no less than a cause, of a high and growing national income.

Thus the American economic revolution of the last quarter-century constitutes a laboratory experiment in which the flow of events has tested on a broad front the Keynesian diagnosis and the Keynesian policies.

The problems of a highly developed economy are different, as we have seen, from those of an economy in the earlier stages of industrial development. The advanced industrial society,

[6] This is the highly important consideration which is overlooked by those who say that all that is needed is to cut government expenditures together with a *corresponding* cut in taxes.

having attained a high level of technology together with entrepreneurial know-how and worker skills, has equipped itself with a vast accumulation of fixed capital. The underdeveloped economy is capital-poor; the advanced country is capital-rich.

No one will deny that the developed economies of Western Europe and North America have reached, after 150 years of technological progress and capital accumulation, a high level of productive capacity. These countries have, moreover, within them the seeds of continued growth. Yet the output of the United Kingdom fell far below her potential throughout the two interwar decades, and in the United States the economy performed disastrously below her capacity for more than a decade before Pearl Harbor. How long must an economy fail notoriously to perform before it is generally admitted that something is seriously lacking?

Now it was Keynes' central thesis that the element that was woefully lacking was *adequate aggregate demand*. The classicals had argued that all that was needed was technology and capital, that the economy itself would automatically generate adequate demand. The interwar experience in the United Kingdom and the deep depression in the United States demonstrated, as conclusively as facts can, that the classical thesis, whatever may have been true of the early days of capitalism, was no longer valid.

But facts convinced no one. Facts alone can never destroy a theory. As President Conant has aptly put it, men strive desperately "to modify an old idea to make it accord with new experiments." An outworn theory will not be abandoned until it has been superseded by a better one. "It takes," says Conant, "a new conceptual scheme to cause the abandonment of an old one." [7]

In his *General Theory of Employment, Money and Interest,*

[7] James B. Conant, *On Understanding Science,* Yale University Press, 1947, pp. 89, 90.

Keynes challenged the view that the modern economic system can be *depended* upon to make automatically the adjustments needed to ensure full use of productive resources. The thing that private enterprise can certainly do efficiently and well is to *produce*. The thing that it cannot be *depended* upon to do well is to ensure adequate aggregate demand.

Just as the decade before the Second World War deepened the conviction that the classicals were wrong, so the last fifteen years have strengthened the conviction that Keynes was right with respect to his positive program. Governments throughout Western Europe, and in the United States, have on an unprecedented scale augmented aggregate demand beyond that generated by private enterprise. And all over the free world, but especially in the United States, we have witnessed what the economy can do when it is put under pressure. Government expenditures, government borrowing, government guarantees and lending operations, government policies in the area of social security, agriculture, public power, rural electrification, securities regulation, deposit insurance, and monetary, banking, and fiscal policies have provided much of the *fuel* needed for the full use of the productive capacity created by technology and capital accumulation.

CHAPTER 3

MONETARY POLICY IN AN ADVANCED ECONOMY

A. The Problem of Inflation

Operating under pressure the American Economy has performed a miracle. The output response to adequate aggregate demand has surprised everyone, and, what is to many still more surprising, it has not led to any such destructive inflation as was feared. Clearly we are not out of the woods in this matter, but the experience of recent years is reassuring. One thing at least is certain. Our economy is equipped with three powerful safeguards against peacetime inflation: (1) Our prodigious capacity to increase production when under pressure; (2) our capacity, both corporate and individual, to save at high-income levels; (3) our demonstrated capacity at responsible fiscal and monetary management. There remains the problem of wages and collective bargaining. This requires, there can be no doubt, statesmanlike action. At all events, I think it is fair to say that experience thus far indicates that the alarmists may well have beaten the drums a little too loudly, and I am happy to note recently a little softer note in the discussion of this very important problem.

A high degree of stability in the value of money must be an important consideration of public policy. Yet we are, I fear, in considerable danger of making a fetish of rigid price stability. This fetish could easily become a serious obstacle to optimum growth and expansion. If we are going to be frightened away by every slight increase in prices, we are likely to fall far below the growth of which we are potentially capable.

We use the term "inflation" far too loosely. The word "inflation" is used to describe the astronomical price increases experienced by Germany after the First World War, and the same word is applied to the comparatively moderate increases in prices in American history. The phrase "inflationary pressures" has often become, I suggest, virtually synonymous with "expansionary forces." Brakes are thereby applied, and output is sacrificed to rigid price stability.

I should like to propose a new definition—one, I hope, which might have some operational value for monetary policy. I suggest that we need a new concept which I propose to call "pure inflation," and I propose to set this concept over against the concept of "price adjustments to output changes." "Pure inflation" (and I emphasize the word "pure"), I should say, is a condition in which prices rise without any appreciable increase in output.

Countries which have suffered in the past from the evils of inflation have typically experienced large price increases with no substantial increase in output. Indeed, in cases of hyperinflation, output has often actually decreased.

There are, to be sure, degrees of pure inflation. And I should like to suggest, to help clarify our thinking, the following general observation. I suggest that at no time in our history, nor indeed in that of any other country, can it be shown that price increases have injured the economy and the general welfare if in the period in question the increase in aggregate output has exceeded percentagewise the increase in prices.

Frederick Mills, of the National Bureau of Economic Research, surveying eighty years of cyclical movements in our history, has shown that, in periods of expansion, for every 1 per cent increase in output we have had 8/10 per cent increase in prices—a 5 to 4 ratio. Professor Mills' short-run ratios of output increases to price increases might, of course, develop against the background either of a long-run downtrend in prices or a long-run uptrend.

I repeat, one does not encounter the condition of inflation in any meaningful sense so long as percentage increases in aggregate output exceed by some margin the percentage increases in the price level.

I should be prepared, in special circumstances, however, to go a bit farther. There are times when a tremendous forward push is urgently needed, when a choice has to be made between permitting a price increase substantially greater than my rule suggests or else foregoing the needed increase in aggregate output.

Consider, for example, the situation in 1946 after the removal of price and wage controls and the cut in wartime taxes. Having chosen to remove the main restraints on consumption (and I assume that political realism forbade any other choice), what then? The only way remaining to keep aggregate demand in check would have been drastic monetary restraint on investment. Would this have been desirable policy? I think not. A rapid transition to full peacetime production required massive investment in plant, equipment, and inventories to make good the accumulated shortages caused by the war. It was a choice of the lesser evil. It did indeed mean a price increase percentagewise considerably greater than the increase in aggregate output. But the massive investment laid the groundwork for a large increase in output later and contributed greatly to the slowing-down of the price movement by 1948.

Following the Second World War we had, as we all know, a considerable price rise. There are those who regard this as simply due to war and postwar mismanagement. I cannot agree. Granted that the controls had to be removed and that taxes had to be cut—that, politically speaking, they could not be continued for a year or so longer—then I think it follows that some considerable price rise was inevitable. This is true because of the accumulated backlog of unfulfilled demand and of postwar shortages. The closets were empty, the shelves were bare; consumers' stocks and business inventories had to be replenished. Under these circumstances price stability could not have been achieved unless indeed we had been prepared to cut employment and income sufficiently to reduce demand to the level of the then available flow of consumers' goods. And a severe cut of this character would have been necessary even though there had been no widespread holdings of liquid savings, since people were quite prepared, in view of the backlog of demand for clothing, household furnishings, automobiles, etc., to spend all of their current income. Any net investment in excess of corporate net saving would under these circumstances have created inflationary pressures.

The path we chose was much to be preferred. It brought indeed a considerable rise in prices, but it gave us full employment and it stimulated a tremendous outpouring of goods which already by the middle of 1947 had drenched the inflationary fires.

Periods of rapid growth have usually also been periods of moderate price increases. In the usual case the price system tends to respond in this manner to rapid expansion. It is not probable that we can achieve in the next twenty years anything like the growth of which we are capable, without some moderate increases in wholesale and consumer prices.

Economists generally tend to exaggerate the evils of moderate price increases. The accumulated savings, it is said, are eaten into. Inflation, it is said, tends to eliminate the sturdy middle class, and it concentrates income in the hands of the lucky few.

These things have indeed always happened in the great

astronomical inflations. And conclusions based on these undoubted facts are then erroneously applied to such price increases as we have experienced in the United States during the
last half-century.

The alleged evils which are typically cited are, in fact, based
on abstractions that have no relevance to conditions as we
actually find them in the United States. We have indeed experienced a considerable price upheaval both in the first quarter
and again in the second quarter of the current century. But
private property continues firmly in the saddle. Savings per
family (after correcting for price changes) are more than
twice as large as in 1925. Urban home ownership has increased
from 45 to 55 per cent. Farm ownership has increased from
58 per cent to 75 per cent. The middle class is stronger than
ever before in our history. There is less inequality in the distribution of income. Adjustments in social-security benefits can
be made and have been made when price changes occur.

In this connection it is well to remember that nothing eats
so dangerously into family savings as deflation and unemployment. On the other hand, even the considerable price increases
we have had since the end of the Second World War have not
wiped out family savings. According to the Home Loan Bank
Board, the accumulated savings, per family, in life insurance,
savings accounts, United States savings bonds, and savings and
loan associations have risen from $2,500 in 1944 to $4,200 in
1954, an increase (after correction for consumer price
changes) of 10 per cent in real purchasing power. I do not
say that we might not have done better had not the aftermath
of the war brought the price increases. But I do say we have
not suffered the serious effects on family savings that are so
often quite irresponsibly alleged.

Thus I conclude that if in the pursuit of rigid price stability
we permit, and even foster, a considerable amount of unemployment, we shall then fail to achieve the growth of which

we are capable. If, fearful of short-run instability, we fail to place the economy under the pressure of an aggregate demand adequate to produce full employment, we shall not even discover what our potentialities for growth are. Under these circumstances we could gradually drift into a condition of stagnation.

B. Historical Perspective

We are living in a century in which the long-run trend in prices has been upward. The two world wars, and to a lesser extent the Korean War, afford, of course, the main explanation.

I think we might gain historical perspective if we take a look at the record of aggregate output and price trends during the last half-century (Table 1). I divide the half-century from 1900 to 1956 into three periods. The first is the quarter-century from 1900 to 1925; the second, the quarter century from 1925 to 1950; the third (by way of comparison) is the short recent period from 1948 to 1956.

TABLE 1. PER CENT INCREASE (PER YEAR) OF OUTPUT AND PRICES *

	1900 to 1925	1925 to 1950	1948 to 1956
Aggregate output	3.5	3.0	4.0
Price index *	3.0	1.5	1.3

* It should be noted that these are *compound* rates of increase and the figures are rounded off at the first decimal point.

The price index is composed of both consumer prices and wholesale prices.

The index numbers are as follows:

	Aggregate output	General index	Consumer index	Wholesale index
For 1925 (1900=100)	240	203	221	185
For 1950 (1925=100)	207	140	137	153
For 1956 (1948=100)	135	111	113	110

With respect to each of these periods I ask two questions: (1) What was the rate of increase of output per annum, and (2) what was the rate of increase of prices per annum, calculated on the compound percentage rate basis? I believe the reader will find the results of this calculation both interesting and instructive.

In the first period, 1900 to 1925, aggregate output increased at the compound rate of 3.5 per cent per annum, prices at the rate of 3 per cent per annum. For the second quarter-century, 1925 to 1950, output increased at the compound rate of 3 per cent per annum, prices at the rate of 1.5 per cent per annum. For the recent short period, 1948 to 1956, output increased at the rate of 4.0 per cent per annum, prices at the rate of 1.3 per cent per annum.

Thus the record with respect to price stability during the last quarter-century is considerably better (contrary to what is commonly believed) than in the first quarter of our century. Prices rose about twice as rapidly per annum in the first quarter of the century.

The greater price revolution of the earlier period also becomes evident when one compares the lowest prewar price years with the postwar price index after prices had settled down. Thus, using the years 1894–1897 as the base, the index, wholesale and consumer combined (for the period in which both are available), stood at 243 in 1923–1925. In the second period, using the low years 1931–1934 as the base, the combined index stood at 200 in 1948–1950.

The great gains in aggregate output, during the last two decades, have been widely distributed—more equally in recent years than ever before. The new price level has not given us, as sometimes in the past, increasing inequality.

Three criteria (all suggested years ago by Professor Pigou) can usefully be applied to test the general health of an economy. They are as follows: (1) Has the per capita real income increased? (2) Have the over-all gains been widely distributed? (3) Has there been adequate capital formation to implement technological progress? The last quarter-century stands up well under these tests.

C. *The Role of Monetary Policy*

Now let me emphasize one thing. We should pursue no fixed goal with respect to price stability. We should emphatically not aim at a constantly rising price level. Nor should we set up the goal of rigid price stability. We should keep our eyes primarily on "maximum production, employment, and purchasing power," the phrase used in our Full-Employment Act.

I should myself hope that over long stretches we could approach our full growth potential at substantially stable prices. I am encouraged in this hope by the record achieved in 1951 to 1956, inclusive.

I suggest that for a rich industrial country the "correct" quantity of money is not any precise fixed amount. It may be anything within a rather wide range. A rich, highly developed country desires and is capable of holding a very large amount of liquid assets in relation to its income. A poor, undeveloped country is not. In a rich country, there is no close relation between the quantity of money and aggregate spending. In a poor country, there is. That is why the quantity theory of money applies quite well to poor countries. The quantity theory has, however, much less relevance for rich, advanced countries.

If the level of economic activity is low, we should actively promote high liquidity and a policy of easy credit. If activity is running very high, the monetary authorities should lean moderately against the inflationary pressures. Monetary policy should make a "modest contribution" toward the containment of inflation, but primary reliance should be placed upon fiscal policy and selective controls.

The monetary authorities should, I believe, follow no rigid formula with respect to the quantity of money. A rich, advanced society does not hold money merely for transaction purposes, and therefore the old velocity concept has become rather meaningless. An advanced society cannot function well without large liquid assets, ready to take advantage of changing investment opportunities and prepared to meet unforeseen contingencies. Such a society cannot prosper without a highly elastic monetary system.

I think we should do well to eliminate, once and for all, the phrase "velocity of circulation" from our vocabulary. Instead, we should simply speak of the ratio of money to aggregate spending. The phrase "velocity of circulation" is, I feel, unfortunate because those who employ it tend to make an independent entity out of it and imbue it with a soul. This little manikin is placed on the stage, and the audience is led to believe that it is endowed with the power of making decisions directing and controlling the flow of aggregate spending. In fact it is nothing of the sort. It is a mere residual.[1] We should get on much better if we substituted the word "ratio." The little manikin would then be forced back into oblivion, where it properly belongs.

As I have tried to indicate, we should have no rigid rule with respect to price stability.[2] We should aim primarily at

[1] The Keynesian analysis has contributed greatly toward an understanding of the factors that determine the residual.

[2] A footnote on another but related matter—the stock-market margin requirements. I should like to raise the question whether any good purpose is ever served by dropping the ratio below 75 per cent. I do not pretend to know the answer, but unless someone can enlighten me to the contrary, I find it difficult to see what purpose, in the general interest, is served by a ratio lower than 75 per cent. And we should not hesitate to raise it to 100 per cent when conditions indicate restraint.

full production and employment, and we should direct our productive energies toward the things most needed.

The Federal Reserve Act, including all its amendments, does not make it the duty or obligation of the System to maintain price stability. Rigid price stability has indeed from time to time been urged upon Congress, and efforts have been made to obtain legislation which would make this a declared policy of the Federal Reserve System. These efforts were rightly resisted. Yet some recent official pronouncements indicate that there is some danger that we are tending to drift in the direction of this rigid dogma.

I do not wish to be misunderstood. I am not advocating price instability. I repeat, the maintenance of reasonable stability in the value of money must clearly remain one of the primary goals of public policy. But as I examine the means of achieving that goal, as encountered in some considerable part of the history of monetary literature, I discover a curious characteristic of monetary reformers, namely, a willingness to introduce a very high degree of instability of wages and of capital values in order to win commodity-price stability.

D. The Dangers of Large Changes in Interest Rates

Prior to the appearance of Keynes' *General Theory* it was the commonly accepted view that wage flexibility was a powerful stabilizing device. Indeed it was argued that the business cycle could be completely eliminated if wages were completely flexible. Now, however, as Professor Pigou himself has said in his contribution to the Keynes *Memoir* issued by Cambridge University, no one can any more contend that a general cut in wages is not deflationary. Complete wage flexibility would give us a violently fluctuating economy. The wage structure is the backbone of the price system. Stable efficiency wages (which means that *money* wages increase at the same rate as increases in productivity) constitute a solid foundation for price stability. We have at long last learned, both from experience and analysis, that we cannot stabilize prices by introducing instability of wages.

Analogous to the thinking which found price stability in wage instability is the theory that stability of the commodity-price level can be achieved by a deliberate fluctuation, even a violent fluctuation, in security prices and capital values.

During most of the nineteenth century this theory, expressed in terms of fluctuations in the rate of interest, had perhaps a certain validity. Formerly wealth assumed primarily two sharply different forms. At one end of the scale was *money*, a perfectly liquid asset. At the opposite end of the scale was *real estate*—homes, shops, small factories, machines—typically owned outright by individual proprietors. Real property was firmly held directly by the owner-operator. There was no day-to-day market for this property, only occasional individual sales. A capital market had not yet developed on any grand scale. Capitalism was still preponderantly in the commercial stage. It was the merchant capitalist who dominated the scene. Trade and commerce were the sources of large fortunes. The *money* market ruled, not the capital market. Commercial banking developed with rapid strides. Trade bills and commercial credit were being monetized by the commercial banks into bank notes and later into demand deposits. The money market made working capital fluid and liquid.

Under the circumstances, sharp fluctuations in the rate of interest affected trade and commerce via their effect on merchants' inventories. There followed a direct and immediate effect on commodity prices. But such fluctuations had very little influence on the value of real estate—property firmly held as equities and not subject to rapid market transfers. The money market, interest rates, and commodity prices—these were the relevant factors in the days when trade and commerce dominated the scene.

As we moved toward the end of the nineteenth century, fixed-capital investment became the dominant characteristic of modern capitalism. Business-cycle theories shifted away from preoccupation with commercial crisis to an analysis of the role of fixed-capital investment in industrial fluctuations. The massive growth of investment in fixed plant and producers' equipment was paralleled by a corresponding growth in the issue of corporate securities. The capital market overshadowed the money market. Investment banking was becoming more lucrative than commercial banking.

Real property was acquiring an undreamed-of liquidity. The stock market made transfers of ownership of fixed capital as easy as the transfer of bills of exchange. All wealth was being capitalized into security values. The owner of a house or a shop never knows from day to day or even from year to year what his property is worth. Now, with the emergence of finance capitalism, the owners even of a great railroad or of giant steel plants can tell from current market quotations exactly what their property is worth.

In this kind of world, primary reliance upon interest-rate policy as a means of stabilizing commodity prices is out of date. In our kind of world, the chief impact of sharp fluctuations in the rate of interest is on capital values.[3] No longer is it possible, as formerly was the case, to influence commodity prices via interest-rate policy without affecting capital values. In our kind of world, the policy of sharp changes in interest rates cannot reach its goal, namely, the stability of commodity prices, without creating a degree of instability in capital values

[3] Cf. Ervin Miller, "Monetary Policy in a Changing World," *Quarterly Journal of Economics*, February, 1956.

commensurate with the vigor of the policy pursued. Now-adays it is not possible, I repeat, to stabilize commodity prices via interest-rate policy without causing instability in capital values.

This is the basic underlying reason why monetary policy is compelled to assume, in modern times, a subsidiary role in the arsenal of stabilization weapons. Central bankers are thoroughly aware of this fact. No central banker is prepared to bring down upon the economy a collapse of capital values. He is perfectly aware that it is no longer possible to penetrate effectively into the area of commodity prices without first making a devastating assault on capital values. This he is not prepared to do, and rightly so. The modern central banker is cautious lest in the effort to stabilize commodity prices he destroy capital values.

Interest-rate policy as a stabilization device is in the modern world not capable of "precision bombing." It is unable to strike at the specific areas that need to be hit. It is a gun-shot method. Capital values are indiscriminately impaired. Areas that ought not be touched are hit no less than those that need to be checked to bring order and stability to expansion. State and local issues confronted with a falling capital market cannot be placed, thereby jeopardizing the stable growth in needed community facilities and services. The industries which are more immediately related to the steady rise in the standard of living, to stable growth and progress, are hit even harder than the speculative industries that feed on a wild, headlong leaping boom. The stable industries are hard hit by higher interest rates, while the high-profit speculative industries ride the swelling waves of a boom virtually unimpeded by even substantial increases in interest rates. Small and growing businesses without large internal sources of funds are hard hit. The rain falls upon the just and the unjust. The method is roughshod.

It seeks to achieve stability by a method which causes general all-round instability of capital values.

E. The Roosa Analysis [4]

Wary of the dangers of sharp fluctuations in the rate of interest, some students of current central-bank techniques (notably Robert V. Roosa, of the New York Federal Reserve Bank) have argued that the very fact that capital values, and especially the government-bond market, play so large a role facilitates the problem of stabilizing the economy. Eschewing drastic changes in interest rates, it is argued that *small* changes, under modern conditions, can have a potent restraining effect in a period of inflationary pressures. Small changes, it is suggested, will operate to induce all potential lenders who happen to hold United States government securities to tighten up on loans to business.

These potential lenders are primarily commercial banks and financial institutions, such as life-insurance companies and savings banks. All these hold large quantities of government securities. The securities in a rich country like the United States can fairly readily be unloaded upon nonfinancial institutions, pension funds, trust funds, and individuals. The funds thus obtained can then be loaned to business. Thus from October, 1954, to October, 1955, commercial banks and financial institutions unloaded $7.9 billion of United States government obligations [5] and employed the funds thus obtained in extending their loans.

Now it is argued that even a moderate tightening-up on

[4] Cf. *Money, Trade, and Economic Growth*, Essays in Honor of John H. Williams, pp. 270–295, The Macmillan Company, 1951.

[5] Nonfinancial corporations took $4.5 billion, state and local governments $1.4 billion, individuals $1.3 billion, and pension funds and other miscellaneous investors $1.2 billion.

reserve balances by Federal Reserve open-market operations, with the consequent small increase in interest rates, will deter financial institutions from unloading their securities. The reasons alleged are as follows: First, selling in a falling bond market means taking capital losses, and this they do not like to show on their books; second, even a slowly falling bond market is likely to be a very thin market,[6] while substantial sales may cause a sharp break resulting in considerable capital losses; third, the securities still held now yield a higher rate of return, and in view of the lag in interest-rate adjustment in the other areas of the interest-rate structure, government securities now become relatively more attractive. For all these reasons it is alleged that potential lenders to business are induced by small increases in interest rates to desist from switching from bonds to loans. Thus, while borrowers may not be appreciably deterred by small increases in interest rates, lenders will be. Federal Reserve restraint is thus, it is alleged, magnified in its potency.

Federal Reserve curtailment not only dries up its own funds but it also dries up the liquid funds held in a rich country by the nonfinancial public—funds which normally are available when financial institutions wish to switch from bonds to loans.

Thus runs the argument. The analysis is quite all right as far as it goes. But in a shifting, dynamic economy there are often cross currents. Anticipating a fall in bond prices, commercial banks and financial institutions may prefer to dump their securities lest large capital losses are suffered later on. They may perhaps be able to make loans at sufficiently higher rates so that a switch from bonds to loans, even at some sacrifice in loss of principal, would be advisable. Should the dumping become

[6] Holders of idle balances become liquidity-conscious and prefer cash to securities. Anticipating a further fall in bond prices, they are wary of capital losses and count on being able to pick up bonds at a lower price later on.

general, it might lead to a demoralized bond market, thereby forcing intervention by the Federal Reserve and thus defeating the initial attempt of restricting the credit base.[7]

The argument that small increases in the rate of interest would deter switching from governments to loans, when all the various cross currents are accounted for, found no support in the events of 1955, already referred to. Throughout this period interest rates were rising, yet commercial banks and financial institutions financed rapidly expanding loans to business mainly from the sale of United States government securities to the investing public.

We are then left with the conclusion that in a rich country like the United States, where much liquid wealth is held by the general public, small changes in the rate of interest can at best represent only a modest deterrent to credit expansion. On the other hand, sharp changes in the rate of interest would create a more dangerous instability than the one it is sought to remedy. What then? Where does this leave us with the problem of stability?

F. A Many-sided Policy

The answer, in my judgment, is plainly that monetary policy can indeed lean against the wind, but it can play only a modest role in a general stabilization program. Primary reliance must be placed upon fiscal policy. A second line of defense is the selective controls of real estate and consumer credit. These are highly sensitive areas in any peacetime inflationary development, and it is only common sense to strike where the pressure is greatest.

[7] Quite another possibility: even small increases in interest rates might tend to become self-defeating by creating a tremendous pressure for funds from borrowers eager to obtain funds before interest rates go still higher or fearful that later on funds may not be available on easy terms.

Primary reliance on fiscal policy, supported by moderate monetary policy, together with selective controls in periods of strong inflationary pressures or whenever real-estate credit and consumer credit are expanding at unusual rates, are, I believe, adequate stabilizing control instruments. In the event that experience shows that more techniques are needed, two measures are available which can powerfully restrain credit without jeopardizing capital values. They are, first, a tax on loans made by commercial banks and financial institutions and, second, a security-reserve requirement ranging from zero to some maximum figure. In the usual case these measures would not be needed, but they might possibly be useful as stand-by controls available for exceptional emergencies or in prolonged periods of inflationary pressures.

The security-reserve device would tend to reinforce powerfully the real-estate and consumer-credit controls, since it tends to drain off the funds flowing into these markets. This is true because the security-reserve plan tends to restrict the switch by commercial banks and financial institutions from United States securities to real-estate and consumer-credit loans.

CHAPTER 4

RECENT MONETARY ISSUES

A. Introductory

The record of postwar central-bank history in the United States points to the conclusion that monetary policy has become only one of many instruments controlling the rate of aggregate spending. Fiscal policy has played the dominant role, with monetary policy and selective controls serving as important supporting measures.

The Hearings of December 6 and 7, 1954, before the Subcommittee on Economic Stabilization (Senator Flanders, Chairman) of the Joint Committee on the Economic Report,[1] provide the third comprehensive survey in recent years on monetary policy. The first was the Douglas Committee Report of 1950; the second, the Patman Committee Report of 1952.

Very much of the ground covered in the December, 1954, hearings is familiar terrain, partly by reason of these earlier investigations. Less familiar issues (though already aired in considerable detail in the Fortieth Annual Report of the Board of Governors of the Federal Reserve System) relate to the policy of the Open Market Committee with respect to its dealings in the government securities market. The hearings are

[1] *United States Monetary Policy: Recent Thinking and Experience*, Hearings before the Subcommittee on Economic Stabilization of the Joint Committee on the Economic Report, 83d Cong., 2d Sess., December 6 and 7, 1954. Washington: United States Government Printing Office, 1954, pp. iv, 331.

enlivened by rather sharp controversy between the Federal Reserve Board and the New York Federal Reserve Bank.

The issues referred to above relate primarily to three matters: (1) Should the Open Market Committee operate in all maturities at its own discretion according to circumstances, or should it confine its operations to the short end of the market? (2) Should the Open Market Committee commit itself "to maintaining orderly conditions in the government security market," or should it limit itself to "correcting a disorderly situation in the government securities market"? (3) Should the System discontinue direct supporting operations during periods of Treasury refinancing?

B. *Restricting Operations to Short-terms*

Adequate liquidity or credit restraint, as the case may be, involves action by the central bank which is bound to affect the prices of government securities. Thus the argument, happily, does not relate to the "phony" question whether or not the government-securities market is "free." A central bank cannot perform its functions without powerfully affecting the prices of government securities. Still it is the aim of the new policy to service the economy with such volume of Reserve bank credit as is needed while disturbing as little as possible the government-securities market.

Perhaps we could all agree that, however important other issues may be, control of the credit base is the gist of monetary management. Wise management, as I see it, should ensure *adequate liquidity* in the usual case and *moderate monetary restraint* (employed in conjunction with other more powerful measures) when needed to check inflation. No doubt others who see no danger in rather violent fluctuations in interest rates (entailing also violent fluctuations in capital values) would put it differently. But at any rate there is agreement, I take it, that the central bank should create a generous dose of liquidity when resources are not fully employed. From this standpoint the *volume* of reserves is of primary importance.

But other important considerations do, in fact, arise, and so the question has to be raised: Where should the central bank enter the market—short-term only or all along the gamut of maturities?

Obviously it would make little difference what maturities were purchased or sold if any change in the volume of reserve money influenced merely the *level* of interest rates, leaving the internal structure of rates unaffected. In short, it would make no difference where the central bank entered the market if there were no lags in the transmission of impulses. In the controversy here under discussion, the Board leans toward the view that the lags are relatively short—new impulses in the short market transmit themselves rapidly to the longer maturities.[2] The New York Federal Reserve Bank officials, on the contrary, lean toward the view that the lags are important.

The experience of 1953–1954 appears in a measure to support the view that impulses at the short end are transmitted fairly rapidly and effectively to the long end of the market. But a longer historical perspective indicates considerable diversity of experience in this matter. And at times the two rates move in opposite directions.

If the central bank limits itself to the short market and if the lags are serious, the mere creation of large reserves may not lower the long-term rate much or soon enough to stimulate investment. Keynes had this in mind when he wrote: "Perhaps a complex offer by the central bank to buy and sell at stated prices gilt-edged bonds of all maturities, in place of the single bank rate for short-term bills, is the most important practical

[2] If there were no lags whatever, it would make no difference what maturities were dealt in. But of course the Board does not hold that there are no lags.

improvement that can be made in the technique of monetary management. . . . The monetary authority often tends in practice to concentrate upon short-term debts and to leave the price of long-term debts to be influenced by belated and imperfect reactions from the price of short-term debts." [3] Keynes, it should be added, wanted the central bank not only to deal in debts of all maturities but also "to deal in debts of varying degrees of risk," i.e., high-grade private securities and perhaps state and local issues.[4]

At the time Keynes was writing we had done very little to make easy money actually available at low long-term rates in the areas that count most. Since then, thanks to FHA, VA, REA, and other lending and guaranteeing operations, we have gone a long way toward making high liquidity per se truly effective in these areas. Operating at the short end, therefore, in view of the development of these institutions, is surely far more effective now than formerly. Thus, from the standpoint of influencing general economic activity, the issue in controversy has perhaps become somewhat less important than when Keynes wrote. Even so, direct intervention in the long-term market, by quickly influencing the mortgage rate, can no doubt contribute much to the effective operation of these new institutional arrangements. Of course if the central bank were prepared to deal directly in private debts of "varying degrees of risk," as Keynes put it, that would be still another matter.

The issue, in addition to the effect on real investment, also involves the impact of the newly announced policy on Treasury refunding and financing operations. In the March 4–5, 1953, meeting of the Open Market Committee a directive was issued which changed Reserve policy. Instead of the earlier

[3] *General Theory*, Harcourt, Brace and Company, Inc., 1936, p. 206.
[4] *Ibid.*, p. 205.

directive which aimed at "maintaining orderly conditions in the government security market," the new directive limited itself "to correcting a disorderly situation in the government-securities market." [5]

This directive is closely related to the decision "to discontinue direct supporting operations during periods of Treasury refinancing with respect both to maturing issues and to new issues being offered, as well as issues comparable to those being offered in exchange" (p. 15).[6]

These directives and policy statements represent a significant change. There is a vast difference between "maintaining orderly conditions" and "correcting a disorderly situation" which has already arisen.

The new directive and policy decision amount to a partial abdication of the Reserve System with respect to one of its functions. Private flotations have the benefit of underwriting support, and one should imagine that a central bank would have as one of its primary functions the obligation to act as the underwriter for Treasury flotations. The abdication is, however, only partial, since the Committee stands ready to correct a disorderly situation. But if the new directive means anything, it means that the Committee would defer action until a disorderly situation has in fact developed, after which it would try to correct it. This indeed is the interpretation placed upon it by Mr. Burgess, who put it this way: "If the market became thoroughly disorderly, they would be pre-

[5] Fortieth Annual Report of the Board of Governors, p. 87.

Note, however, the firm statement, p. 22 of the Hearings, that the Open Market Committee "would stand ready to intervene with direct purchases, sales or swaps in any sector where market developments took a trend that the Committee considered was adverse to high level economic activity."

[6] All page references, unless otherwise indicated, are to the December, 1954, Hearings.

pared to go in and do whatever was necessary to straighten the matter out" (p. 177). And the Board itself states emphatically that "the market would have to be clearly disorderly before such intervention would occur" (p. 23).

The Board officials advance the hypothesis (a matter which should especially interest theoretical economists) that the new directives will in fact tend to provide a smoother, more orderly market. On grounds of general reasoning one might suppose that a policy directive aiming at "maintaining an orderly market" would tend to (a) counteract any abnormally disturbing events that might upset the market, (b) minimize risk and uncertainty, and (c) promote a smooth, well-functioning market. No, say the Board officials, the market tends to regard Federal Reserve operations in the long-term markets as arbitrary interference—artificial intervention which increases the risks and uncertainties with which dealers must contend.

The notion that Federal Reserve intervention in the market has the effect of increasing risk and uncertainty is certainly one of the most curious arguments I have ever encountered.[7] And it is particularly remarkable coming from the Reserve authorities themselves. Federal Reserve intervention, so says the Board, has a disruptive and disorganizing effect on the market (pp. 15–26).

We are told that the new directives—the shift from "maintaining orderly conditions" to "correcting disorderly situations" and the decision to confine operations to the short end —were issued "to remove a disconcerting degree of uncertainty that existed at that time among market intermediaries and financial specialists." These uncertainties related to trans-

---

[7] Intervention by the System tends, the Board says, to drive dealers out of the market. They tend to become mere brokers.

One might indeed think that dealers would tend to become mere brokers in a rigidly pegged market. But this is not the case under consideration here. An orderly market is not a riskless market. There remains ample scope for speculative profits by dealers.

actions "outside the short end of the market." The effect was "to limit significantly the disposition of market intermediaries and financial specialists to take positions, make continuous markets, or engage in arbitrage in issues outside the short end of the market." Reserve intervention, which "would often seem capricious" to market intermediaries, "constituted a market risk." These uncertainties "would tend to perpetuate a condition of thin markets and sluggish adjustment as between sectors of the market." Operating experience since June, 1953, shows, it is alleged, that the market "has become progressively broader, stronger and more resilient" (p. 16). In the Report of the Ad Hoc Subcommittee of November 12, 1952, the pet phrase "depth, breadth and resiliency" is used no less than sixteen times (pp. 257–289), and it is frequently used in other submissions of the Board.

Against this the New York Federal Reserve Bank remarks somewhat dryly as follows: The "idea that the dealers will be encouraged to take larger positions and to make broader and firmer markets,[8] once the System gives assurance that it will stay out of all but the short-term sector of the market, deserves scrutiny. . . . Fear of adverse trends, or uncertainty as to what the trend is likely to be, is the predominant reason for thin markets, rather than apprehensions concerning System intervention in particular sectors to limit price movements" (p. 310).

"It is quite likely that in most circumstances the System will be able to attain its policy objectives by operating only in the market for Treasury bills and other short-term securities. It is at least possible, however, that on some occasions the System might better be able to effectuate its policies by operating in

[8] The reader will note the ill-concealed amusement of the writers of the New York Bank's reply, derived from quoting on every possible occasion the sonorous phrase "depth, breadth and resiliency of the market," of which the Ad Hoc Committee is so fond.

other sectors of the market—even the longest maturities—
depending upon the economic conditions then prevailing."
The "accord" has as its objective the freeing of the System, not
the complete withdrawal from the long-term market.[9] In
most circumstances when intervention in the long-term market was considered appropriate, short-term operations would
either not have been effective or would have needed larger-
scale operations than credit policy would justify (p. 311).

Facilities for market arbitrage, the New York Bank believes,
are not sufficiently developed to ensure a smooth flow of reactions throughout the longer sectors of the market. Arbitrage
operations are extremely uncertain. The record shows that
little may be dependably expected. Indeed under the impact
of disequilibrating forces the two rates may well move against
each other (pp. 311–312).

A common-sense view of the matter, I suggest, could perhaps be stated as follows: Experience proves that Reserve
intervention in the market has been on balance stabilizing—
not arbitrary or disturbing. Such intervention, tending to
smooth over the rough spots, promotes widespread confidence
in the government-securities market and is welcomed by all
except possibly the wildest speculators. Such a market is not a
pegged market, and there is ample scope for operators to pit
their intelligence against market risks and thereby (if successful) make a good profit.

Even in the days prior to March, 1951, the market usually
fluctuated over a considerable range above par. The range of
fluctuations was of course narrowed by the support policy.
Following the accord, the possible and probable range of
fluctuations, even though the Federal Reserve continued to
maintain an orderly market, has been wider.

[9] At one point the Board refers to *traditional central banking policy*,
but this effort to lean on authority did not impress the New York
Federal Reserve Bank (see p. 311).

A continuously maintained orderly market (but not a pegged market) makes the best of two worlds—elimination of arbitrary and disturbing fluctuations, on the one side, and, on the other, the free play of investor judgment by dealers, financial institutions, banks, and the public coping with the more normal risks and uncertainties inherent in a dynamic and changing world—a world, however, in which government intervention in all sorts of ways plays a stabilizing role. (Witness, for example, the stabilizing governmental policies listed in the President's Economic Report of January, 1955.)

Monetary policy can operate on two planes: (1) controlling the credit base—the volume of reserve balances—and (2) changing the interest-rate structure. The Federal Reserve has now backed away from the second. The Treasury emphasized in these Hearings that this is its special bailiwick. It supports, so it asserts, the System's lead, by issuing short-terms or long-terms, as the case may be, according to whether the Federal Reserve is trying to expand or to contract credit. The Federal Reserve, we are told, leads the way by open-market operations in the short market; the Treasury then backs up the System by issuing the appropriate maturity, thus directly influencing the *structure* of interest rates.

One gets the impression that the Treasury testimony at various intervals in these Hearings seems to be more or less self-contradictory. At one point (pp. 206–207) Secretary Humphrey is eager to explain that when the Treasury offers a new issue, it must start where the market (including any action independently made by the Federal Reserve) fixes the rate.[10]

---

[10] I pass over the unfortunate analogy which the Secretary made between the Treasury's position and that of the farmer's wife who sells a few dozen eggs, since this may well have been an inadvertent comment which it would be unfair to pin too firmly on the Secretary.

But the question may well be asked whether pronouncements made during and after the campaign with respect to a program to fund the public debt and the need for a harder money policy with higher rates

Later in the testimony, however, it was explained that the Treasury can powerfully influence the market and that in fact, during the current recession, the Treasury has effectively contributed to monetary ease by placing main reliance on short-terms in its financing operations. By pursuing this policy, it has not competed with the placement of private securities, and it has thus helped to bring down the long-term rate. The Treasury, by switching from long-term to short-term issues, or vice versa, can thus exercise a strong influence on the money and capital markets.

Thus, from the testimony of the Federal Reserve and of the Treasury it appears that we now have (whether by accident or design) a division of monetary management between the two agencies—a sort of informal cartel arrangement. The Federal Reserve limits itself to control of the *volume* of credit by operating exclusively in the short end of the market.[11] The Treasury shifts from short-term to long-term issues when monetary restraint is called for, and back to short-term issues when expansion is desired.

The Treasury says (p. 161) that the Federal Reserve commands and the Treasury obeys. In February–May, 1953, it would appear to an outsider that the Treasury, moving strongly out on long-terms, led the way, with the Federal Reserve, shall we say, at least not effectively resisting! But when this policy got us into trouble, the Federal Reserve quickly seized the reins and dramatically got us out of the woods with its policy of "active ease." For this action the System certainly deserves full credit.

---

of interest to cope with inflation would not inevitably be very powerful factors influencing the market, and whether in fact this was not indeed the case in May, 1953, when the ill-fated 3¼ per cent was offered.

[11] The Federal Reserve does, of course, control the rediscount rates charged by the Federal Reserve Banks.

C. *Exaggerated Claims by Monetary Authorities*

The statements submitted by the Federal Reserve authorities in these Hearings relate to other matters, and with respect to some of them I do not feel altogether happy. The following are some of the points which I feel deserve critical consideration.

Before making these comments I should like to say that in my view the record of responsible management by the monetary authorities during the period following the Second World War (with the rare and brief exceptions noted below) is on balance an admirable one. What I have to say relates not to policy (except for the rare occasions noted) but rather to the *claims* made and the nature of the arguments supporting these claims. This is a matter which, unless corrected, could easily lead to serious consequences for monetary management.

1. I believe it is fair to say that the Reserve authorities are far too eager to claim undue credit for the stability of prices which we have enjoyed since February–March, 1951. The position taken by the Board is not without danger, since Congress might well draw the conclusion that if monetary policy is indeed as powerful as indicated, nonmonetary measures (measures which politicians are often reluctant to enact) are either unnecessary or may be drawn upon lightly. It is true that nonmonetary factors are indeed mentioned in the Board's statement, but are they given their proper weight?

Thus, for example, I believe it can plausibly be argued that by far the most important factor bringing the Korean price rise to a halt was the thumping cash surplus in the first half of calendar year 1951. Another immensely important factor (probably far more important than the mild monetary restraint actually imposed) was the spontaneous cessation of panic buying by both business and consumers—the backwash from the inventory spree[12] and the consumer grab for durables in the first flush of frantic expenditures aroused by the Korean crisis. In addition, producers responded magnificently to the increased demand. And besides the monetary restraint imposed after March, 1951, there were the direct controls introduced in January and the selective real-estate and consumer-credit controls.

Surely it is incumbent upon the monetary authorities to make a judicious assessment of all the factors involved. To exaggerate the role of monetary policy can easily have the effect of fostering dangerous illusions which might militate against a well-balanced program.

2. I feel that the Board has presented a rather sorry statistical case to show that powerful monetary restraint was in fact imposed after March, 1951. Let me hasten to say that I do not doubt that monetary restraint was indeed imposed and that such restraint was helpful. I believe, however, that the restraint was very moderate, as it indeed should have been under the circumstances. I believe that the very large bank-credit expansion which in fact did occur after March, 1951, was amply justified by the prodigious growth and expansion of the economy. I approve of the policies pursued. I am only criticizing the arguments advanced in this statement.

What does this statement do? It seeks to prove statistically that powerful monetary restraint was, in fact, imposed by showing that the rate of increase in bank credit after March,

[12] I recall an illuminating statement made by one of the Länder central bankers in West Germany in the summer of 1951. He was detailing to me the effectiveness of the stringent credit contraction imposed by the Bank deutscher Länder in February, 1951. Inadvertently, however, he gave much of his case away by dropping the following comment: "But of course much the same decline in bank credit would have occurred anyway, because businessmen generally had heavily overextended themselves with excessive inventories, and after February, 1951, they were spontaneously running to cover."

1951, was slower than the rate of increase during the eight months of panic buying following the Korean bombshell! This is indeed a remarkable performance. Every statistician knows that it is incumbent upon him to use a base that can reasonably be justified. By no stretch of the imagination can the eight-month panic buying be regarded as a reasonable base.

If this were the only period available for comparison, that would be one thing. But the question here relates to the degree of monetary restraint *after* and *before* the accord. Now, we had at least four years of experience before Korea. A comparison could easily have been made with respect to the rate of increase of credit, of money supply, etc., in the pre-Korea period with the post-accord period. For example, the reader might well ask, why was not the chart on page 28 carried back to 1946? Had this been done (as I shall show later), the statistical demonstration would have led to a completely different conclusion.

In point of fact, no statistical comparison, neither the one used nor the one which I have suggested above, could really answer the question whether a strongly effective monetary restraint was in fact exercised after the accord. The reason is this: Earlier conditions, both before Korea and during the buying spree, were fundamentally different from the post-accord period. A comparison of rates of increase of credit per se proves nothing. Indeed, if we were to rely on this criterion alone, we would have to conclude (see below) that the period June, 1946–June, 1950, witnessed a monetary restraint far more effective than that achieved after the accord.

3. I am especially unhappy about the *implication* that the price stability which we have enjoyed since February–March, 1951 (and about which everyone is justifiably happy) could easily have been purchased for the entire postwar period (1945 to the present) had we only adopted the famous accord earlier. This view, which permeates the Board's statement, represents

a vast oversimplification. Possibly it might have been advisable to have made the accord earlier than we did (say in 1949, when it would have had no immediate effect but would have been available for later use).[13] Nevertheless, had the hands of the Federal Reserve been thus freed prior to Korea, it is highly questionable that the history of price movements since 1949 would have been substantially different. No tolerable monetary restraint could effectively have curtailed the upswing of prices induced by the unprecedented expenditures aroused by the Korean explosion. And, much as it is to be regretted that Congress had not given the Board permanent stand-by control over real-estate and consumer credit, does anybody really believe that even those direct measures could have had much effect in those eight months of panic buying? Had *all* our control measures (including tax measures) been in stand-by order, we could doubtless have moderated somewhat the Korean price spurt. Later on, of course, when the three new tax laws began to take effect, when the supply situation had radically changed, and when the most persistent purchasers had already been satisfied, the whole situation became more manageable. Within the pattern of those changed circumstances, moderate monetary restraint, together with selective controls, was indeed able, after March, 1951, to play a role.

Nor do I believe that we would have escaped the considerable price inflation of 1946–1947 had the hands of the Reserve authorities not been tied with respect to the support of long-

[13] As late as 1949 the Board and the Treasury were in entire accord over the policy not to permit the long-terms to fall below par. Said the Chairman of the Board on May 11, 1949: "In retrospect, I am certain that our action in support of the government's securities market was the right one. . . . I am convinced that we could not have abandoned our support position during the period without damaging repercussions on our entire financial mechanism as well as seriously adverse effects on the economy generally." (*Monetary Policy and the Management of the Public Debt*, Joint Committee on the Economic Report, 82d Cong., 2d Sess., pt. I, p. 360.)

terms at par. The postwar cut in individual taxes and the removal of price, wage, and other controls in 1946—these Acts of Congress, whatever we may think of them, do not here come into question—did away once and for all with any really effective restraint on consumers.[14] Under these circumstances the prevention of price inflation simmered down to a restraint on investment. Now this of course is exactly the area in which monetary restraint is most effective. Having in mind, however, the vast backlog of demand for business plant and equipment and the pressing shortage of housing, together with the volume of liquid assets on hand, is it really credible that a drastic curtailment of investment would have been tolerated any more than the continuation of wartime taxation and controls?

In the final analysis, of course, the then prevailing excess of demand was confronted with a limited supply of productive resources, and the inflation served as a sort of impersonal rationer of scarce goods. But the powerful upsurge of demand also served to increase output. And the enormous volume of investment in plant and equipment prepared the way for the miracle of production which followed.

It would seem that a brief survey might well have been made of action taken prior to the accord—action which was certainly not altogether ineffective. This kind of thing has indeed been done admirably by President Sproul of the New York Bank in his chapter in the volume in honor of John H. Williams.[15] Here one finds a thoroughly objective discussion. For example, when Mr. Sproul relates the role of financial institutions as suppliers of funds in 1947–1948—funds derived in part by large sales of government securities to the Reserve banks—he is careful to note that such purchases of bonds by

[14] General monetary restraint (exclusive of control of consumer credit) is notoriously weak with respect to consumption.

[15] *Money, Trade, and Economic Growth: In Honor of John Henry Williams*, The Macmillan Company, 1951.

the Federal Reserve banks were more than offset by sales of short-terms, so that there was, in fact, a net reduction in the total holdings of securities by the System. He notes that, while such problems were causing concern, in reality the situation was not critical in view of the Treasury's cash surplus and other factors. He notes the raising of the short-term rates in the spring and summer of 1948, and as a central banker he might have credited the decline in prices which began in August of that year to these interest-rate changes. But he modestly (and I think wisely) refrains from doing so.

Addressing himself to those who demanded the use of "almost unlimited powers to raise the discount rates and to sell government securities in the open market," Sproul warns that this "sort of action would not be the answer to the situation which existed in 1946–1948." It might indeed have been effective in "bringing about a contraction, but at a cost in fiscal and financial disorder, and in terms of reduced production and employment which few would have wanted to contemplate. General monetary controls, if used drastically enough, work through a restriction of production." Nonetheless, while refusing to make extravagant claims, he concludes that monetary control and debt management "can play an important *though modest* role in promoting stability in our economy." [16]

4. One gets the impression from the Board's submissions in these Hearings that in the pre-accord days money and bank credit ran wild. Attempts at credit restraint had, we are told, "*diminishing* results as *mounting* sales of securities to the Federal Reserve by banks and other holders made funds abundantly and cheaply available" (p. 4).[17] The reader gets a picture of a flood of sales to the Federal Reserve and a rapidly

[16] Italics are mine. This phrase, as a description of the proper role of monetary policy, should, I believe, be attributed to Professor Williams himself.

[17] Italics are mine.

mounting money supply. Again, one reads that the Open Market account performed the function of "making continuous markets for most maturity sectors even including the very short end of the market." The result, we are told, was a "spiral of costs and prices." And again: "This inflationary process was stopped early in 1951 when the Federal Open Market Committee discontinued pegging the prices of United States government securities" (p. 20). Finally, the following: "The facts are that debt was monetized *in volume*,[18] and that the country suffered a serious inflation until the Federal Open Market Committee abandoned the pegs" (p. 278).

Now the facts are, however, quite otherwise than here stated. There occurred no "mounting" monetization of the debt. On the contrary, Federal Reserve holdings were $5.1 billion *less* in June, 1950, than in December, 1946. The debt was not "monetized in volume." The banking system held $14.0 billion less bonds in June, 1950, than in December, 1946, while the nonbank public held $13.5 billion more.[19] The money supply did not increase. Currency plus demand deposits stood at $110.2 billion in June, 1950, and at $110.0 billion in December, 1946. We did not have continuous inflation in the pre-accord period. Wholesale prices in June, 1950, stood at the same level as in September, 1947, a period of nearly three years. Loans and

[18] Italics are mine.

[19] "Debt monetization refers to the creation of money by the banking system in exchange for title to debt instruments. . . . Insofar as the commercial banks or the Federal Reserve Banks acquire existing debt, government or private, from the non-bank public, the deposits of the commercial banks (or currency in circulation) are correspondingly increased" (see *Monthly Review*, Federal Reserve Bank of New York, February, 1955).

This is a good statement. Nevertheless, it should be emphasized that the heart of the matter relates to monetization of "high-powered" money through the sale of securities to the Federal Reserve banks. Such sales increase member-bank reserve balances and enlarge the credit base.

investments of commercial banks remained stationary from 1946 to 1948 but rose moderately before Korea. Member-bank reserve balances stood at $16.1 billion in December, 1946, and at $16.3 billion in June, 1950.[20] Money and bank credit were not running wild as Table 1 discloses.

TABLE 1. CURRENCY, DEPOSITS, AND BANK EARNING ASSETS, 1946–1950
($ BILLION)

	December, 1946	June, 1948	June, 1950
Currency plus demand deposits, adjusted	$110.0	$108.3	$110.2
U.S. securities held by comm. banks and F.R. banks	97.9	86.0	83.9
U.S. securities held by F.R. banks	23.4	21.4	18.3 *
Loans and investments of comm. banks	114.0	113.9	121.8

* Offsetting the decline in securities, the gold assets of the F.R. Banks increased from $18.4 billion in December, 1946, to $23.0 billion in June, 1950.

It would be difficult to find statements more misleading than those cited above. The reader is not told that the peg on the short-term was removed four years before the accord. He is not told that the support of the long-term was a *floor* support, not a fixed peg. He is not told that during most of the period the long-terms were selling above the support price. He is not told that the money supply in fact did not increase from 1946 to June, 1950. He is not told that wholesale prices were falling for about two years before Korea. The reader is led to believe

[20] Reserve requirements were 20, 20, and 14 per cent, respectively, for central reserve city, reserve city, and country banks in 1946; and 22, 18, and 12 per cent, respectively, in June, 1950.

that there was a continued spiral of rising costs and prices all through this period. Nor is the reader informed that the price spurt following Korea was stopped a month before the accord —the weekly index reaching the peak figure on February 13, 1951.

The highly stable supply of money and credit in the pre-Korean period is to be explained partly by the moderate credit needs of business in view of the high postwar liquidity of business. It is, however, to be explained partly by highly responsible management by the monetary authorities within the limits of such powers as they possessed.

Clearly the debt was not being monetized in volume despite the Federal support of long-terms at par. How does one explain this? Why did not everyone rush to turn in his "governments" for cash?

There are several good reasons.[21]

a. Throughout most of this period we had a substantial cash surplus which was effectively used to retire bank-held debt, and especially Federal Reserve holdings.

b. The peg on the short-term rate was removed in mid-1947.

c. During most of the period from 1946 to Korea the prices of long-term United States securities were sufficiently above par so that the Federal support did not in fact come into play. In short, the strong bond market gave conclusive proof of the fact that the public preferred bonds to cash. Thus the Federal Reserve was not flooded with bonds.

d. Contrary to the view which one so often encounters— here I do not refer to the Board—that the public cannot be trusted with assets which can easily be converted into money, the facts are quite otherwise, at least in rich countries like the United States. The stable volume of savings bonds held by the

[21] Some of these are discussed in *Monthly Review* of the Federal Reserve Bank of New York, February, 1955, p. 19.

public throughout the postwar period and the growth in savings deposits are very impressive. So long as current incomes remained high, as was indeed the case in the postwar period, there was no pressure to sell bonds for cash. Moreover, business corporations held large cash balances following the war, and this also was a factor.[22]

5. In view of the supposed "newly acquired" independence of the Federal Reserve from Treasury domination, the Board's support in these Hearings of the much criticized Treasury policy from February to May, 1953, is somewhat surprising. Outside of the Treasury and the Board, it is hard to find anyone who is prepared to defend this policy. And the Board's support, strangely enough, appears to be much stronger, *after the event*, than it was at the time.

The Treasury defends its policy by the claim that dangerous inflationary pressures demanded a change-over to a much tougher, hard-money policy. Board statements in the December, 1954, Hearings support this view. But the pronouncements at the time were far milder. Thus on February 20, 1953, the Board reduced the margin requirements from 75 per cent to 50 per cent. This action was taken (it was explained—see p. 83, *Fortieth Annual Report*) because by "February, 1953, inflationary pressures had moderated." Similarly, in the March 4–5, 1953, Record of Policy Actions of the Federal Open Market Committee, it was explained (*Fortieth Annual Report*, p. 87–

[22] While the monetization of the debt was held in check up to the time of Korea, was there not a rush to monetize when this crisis broke?

Even here, I think, evidence to this effect is not convincing. Federal Reserve Bank holdings did indeed increase from June, 1950, to March, 1951. But this increase in holdings by the Federal Reserve banks can surely not be divorced from the unfortunate effect of the "discord" (between the Reserve authorities and the Treasury from August, 1950 to March, 1951) which seriously disorganized the market for government securities, making it necessary for the System to take refunding issues which, in the climate of uncertainty then prevailing, could not readily be placed.

88) that "for some months, credit policy had been devoted toward the general objective of keeping the supply of credit and money adjusted to the needs of a growing and high-level economy in which there was no immediate evidence of price inflation. . . . Under the conditions that existed during 1952, when there was strong demand for credit from both private and government sectors of the economy, this policy resulted in bank reserve positions being under pressure throughout most of the year. Bank credit expansion . . . was thus kept within bounds in order to discourage inflationary developments." It was the consensus of that March, 1953, meeting that just as in 1952 there was still reason to feel concern about the possibility of inflationary developments. "The Committee agreed, therefore, that it would pursue a policy which would maintain *about the same degree of restraint* on credit expansion that had been followed in recent preceding months, a policy consistent with a stable price level and a high level of economic activity" (p. 88, italics mine).

These quotations do not indicate that either the Board or the Committee saw *at the time* any *new* developments that called for a *change* in monetary policy.

The Treasury alleged that the inventory build-up was inflationary. In point of fact the build-up of inventories in the last half of 1952 and early 1953 was a necessary development following the termination of the steel strike. Without this build-up the vast expansion of production could not have occurred. This was not therefore simply a speculative build-up. It was a necessary prerequisite to increased output.

It is, of course, true that even necessary inventory accumulations must end, but this in itself should be no cause for alarm unless stocks were built up to a point that was clearly excessive. This was not the case in this period. The average ratio of inventories to sales from 1948 to 1952, inclusive, was 1.61. The ratio stood at 1.60 in February, 1953, and fell to

1.59 and 1.57 in March and April, respectively.[23] Not until
sales declined rather sharply in August did the ratio rise. The
August rise was a case of *involuntary* inventory accumulations
due to sales falling below expectations.

The wholesale price index, which had averaged 110.5 in the
last quarter of 1952, fell to 109.8 in the first quarter of 1953
and stood at 109.4 in April. Yet despite these facts, and the
moderate pronouncements *at the time* which indicated no *new*
concern about inflationary pressures, the Reserve authorities
in the Hearings of December, 1954, supported the Treasury
view that powerful *new* inflationary forces justified the ill-
fated hard-money venture.

A far more reasonable explanation—one which can scarcely
be effectively denied—is that the policy was dictated by pre-
conceived notions of debt management. The policy pursued
was clearly indicated by public pronouncements made before
the Administration took office, during and after the campaign.
The fiction that the action taken was simon-pure flexible
monetary policy is (one gathers from what one hears and
reads) scarcely believed by anyone outside of the official
family of the Treasury and the Reserve Board. These Hearings
themselves bear witness to this fact.

[23] See *Economic Indicators.*

CHAPTER 5

THE MAGNA CARTA
OF ECONOMIC PLANNING

A. Economics for the General Public

Sometime during the war years a small group of economists gathered at the home of Eugene Meyer to discuss the following problem: Could a program be launched (perhaps with the cooperation of leading newspapers) designed to raise the level of public understanding of economic affairs? After considerable discussion there was general agreement that each of the proposals made presented insuperable difficulties, not the least of which was the difficulty of ensuring anything approaching a balanced yet incisive presentation of the different viewpoints held by competent people. The project was abandoned. For one thing, where would we find the columnists equal to the task? Sumner Slichter had not yet displayed his wares, and even now there is but one Slichter!

Now, it is my view that the Economic Reports of the President, with the help of the Council of Economic Advisers, and the Reports of the Joint Committee on the Economic Report have filled in significant measure a serious gap in our educational media. These documents are available to any high-school or college teacher even in the most backward part of the country. They are put under the noses of journalists, editors, and radio and television commentators and newscasters. The President is put on record for all to read. And if one doesn't like the economic philosophy of the President, he can look up the Minority Report of the Joint Committee. One can give himself a fairly good practical education in applied economics by spending a few hours each week studying these reports. They constitute in effect a popular-economics textbook [1] which has the great merit of dealing with vital, practical issues and of being strictly current. Even Samuelson's famous textbook on Economics, with triennial editions, is not quite that up to date!

To the Reports must be added the Hearings before the Joint Economic Committee. Many of these hearings are, in fact, high-level seminars in which different points of view are debated by university, business, trade-union, and farm economists, with senators and congressmen asking penetrating questions. The Employment Act of 1946 has truly set in motion a great educational process.

This particular bit of machinery is indeed only a part, though perhaps the most important part, of a more general process. Everything considered, it is my distinct feeling that we have moved a long way from the generally prevailing economic illiteracy of a generation ago to at least a modicum of economic literacy. The revolutionary increase of trained economists in the government service, compared with twenty years ago, has made its contribution. State papers and the speeches of leading government officials reflect this change. Pious platitudes face a tougher competition for space than formerly, though many still retain lusty qualities. There remains, nonetheless, a not inconsiderable gap between the body of current scientific economic knowledge and the prevailing folklore.

[1] On a more technical plane is the notable 1953 Council Report. Special credit is given in this Report to the highly competent staff members. In a sense this Report is a textbook on the methodology of economic programming.

B. Critical Periods for the Employment Act Setup

The machinery setup in the Employment Act is not only of educational value; it is an instrument for economic planning. The Act makes it mandatory upon the President to set forth the targets (levels of employment, production, and purchasing power) needed and also a program for carrying out the policy of the Act. Thus a public forum is provided in which the Congress, and indeed the entire nation, participate—a forum in which all of us together assess where we are and where we are going.

The Employment Act of 1946 has had to face two critical periods. The first was the initial launching of a wholly new venture in an atmosphere of widespread suspicion. The second was the building of a bridge between an outgoing and incoming Administration. In my view, professional economists everywhere, and all those who are concerned that light and knowledge be applied to the utmost feasible extent to our public affairs, should be profoundly grateful that these two critical periods are safely behind us. For this I feel, and I am sure that most of my readers will agree, that Edwin Nourse as chairman of the Council during the first critical period, and Arthur Burns as chairman during the second, deserve very great credit. Also, through the formative years the appointment of a highly competent staff was crucial. In this connection special note should be made of the work of Gerhard Colm and Walter Salant and, in more recent years, the notable job of building up the work of the Joint Committee by Grover Ensley.

We are now, I believe, past the more serious danger points. The Employment Act, and all it stands for, is at long last a firmly intrenched institution. It is in a way the cornerstone to the reconstruction which has remade and enormously strengthened the American economy during the last quarter-century.

C. *A Cynic's Appraisal*

We must, however, not exaggerate what has been accomplished under the Employment Act. A cynic could argue, not altogether without reason, that the miracle of performance of the American Economy in the entire postwar period is pure accident. This cynic, strangely enough, could even be a good Keynesian! He could argue that the one new factor (not formerly present or at least not present continuously for so long a period) which accounts for this miracle was an incredibly high and sustained level of *aggregate demand*. He could argue that this was clearly not due, on the one hand, to the automatic functioning of the economy running on its own steam, since all through the period there were gigantic Federal budgets, even in the relatively peacetime years preceding Korea; and, on the other hand, he could argue that it had little or nothing to do with the Employment Act, since the major decisions were *forced* upon us. We had no choice. We did not have to go through the painful process of reaching agreement on a truly peacetime program.

Our cynic could, moreover, argue that our remarkably successful adjustments to the problems created by this high-pressure economics were due to fortuitous luck and not to scientific administration guided by expert economic knowledge. The famous tax cut of April, 1948, was exactly what was needed, but it was passed for the wrong reasons. The large veterans' dividend of the first quarter of 1950 was just what was wanted to help lift us out of the 1949 recession, but its timing had nothing to do with business forecasting.

The pay-as-you-go taxes of 1950–1951 must, however, be credited in part at least to an awakened appreciation of the true role of fiscal policy. Much credit is also due the Federal Reserve for the swift change-over to monetary ease of early 1953. And the tax reductions of 1953–1954 reflected, I believe, in no small measure the revolution in economic thinking, though our cynic could, of course, point to the fact that most of them were already on the books!

Also, our cynic could point out that much, if not most, of what was urged with hortatory fervor in the Economic Reports of the President was never passed by Congress, and that not infrequently Congress was right.

Our cynic, looking ahead (and strongly conscious of his Keynesian background), might well be skeptical of the future. He might have serious doubts that we shall do very well even under the Employment Act. He may argue that we have never yet had any real test. He may observe that we agree on big problems only when a major crisis is upon us. When the crisis is past, we fall apart and quarrel. Foreign economic aid is voted when Russia infiltrates Czechoslovakia or when Bulganin and Khrushchev visit India. Otherwise economic aid faces tough going. So also with all the really big programs needed to fully supplement the purposes of the Employment Act.

Our cynic might perhaps admit that really difficult choices are, in fact, not likely to confront us. The cold war will be upon us for a long time, and this makes us pull together. The larger the Gross National Product grows in relation to the public debt, the more we may be willing to cut taxes drastically when necessary to maintain full employment. And our cynic might also agree that the longer the cold war lasts, the more unbearable will become the seriously accumulating deficiencies in our infant welfare state which badly needs nourishment for the healthy growth of its schools, hospitals, roads, and community services. The demand for increased civil expenditures will surely cumulate. Social priorities will at long last demand attention.

D. The Joint Economic Committee

Perhaps the most significant single event of the entire experience under the Employment Act was the unanimous Report of the Joint Committee on the Economic Report in 1954, and repeated again in 1955. Up to this time the Joint Committee reports had been largely partisan documents, not infrequently (particularly in the Minority reports) disclosing a basic distrust of positive governmental programs to maintain full employment. When the Eisenhower Administration came into power, proclaiming with reiterated emphasis its determination to use its vast powers to the limit to promote the goals set forth under the Employment Act, all this was changed. The Joint Committee as a body henceforth was solidly behind the Employment Act and broadly sympathetic with the measures needed to implement it.

But this was not all. The Joint Committee now began to assume an independently positive role. Even in the 1954 Report, when the Republicans constituted the majority, the Joint Committee was critical of the President for not going far enough in the positive measures proposed. The Joint Committee now began more and more to develop a program of its own. It set going very extensive hearings on monetary policy, foreign economic policy, tax policy, economic stabilization, economic statistics, and low-income families.[2] The Joint Committee, which many had thought to be sort of a "fifth wheel" in the Employment Act machinery, now began to take the lead. The elaborate and highly competent hearings of the

[2] The Committee had indeed been active in some of these areas earlier, but this renewed activity represented a more vigorous and positive approach.

Committee are increasingly disclosing fresh materials of great significance. These contributions indeed bid fair to outrun in importance the materials appearing in the President's Economic Reports.

E. The Role of the Council of Economic Advisers

One important matter of procedure (for years a subject of controversy) has at last been settled, in my judgment, rightly. It concerns the relation of the Council to the Economic Report.

Earlier the hope was nourished by some that the Council could somehow play the role of an Economic Supreme Court or Independent Economic Mentor dispensing "economic truth" above the din of political battle. This hope inspired the early Special Reports of the Council and perhaps also the later division of the Economic Report into (a) the President's Report and (b) the Council's Annual Economic Review.

The earlier view of the Council, as potentially an independent entity, shifted, under Keyserling's chairmanship, to the view that the Council should perform as an integral part of the *political* machinery and should indeed play a leading role as the chief economic advocate for the Administration in power. It is, I think, a fact that there is a widespread opinion throughout the country that this placed the Council in an unnecessarily controversial position.

When the Council was reorganized under Burns' chairmanship, the separate economic reports were, I think wisely, abandoned. The Council receded measurably into the background. It restricted itself more nearly, though not quite exclusively, to the role of assisting and advising the President.

There remains a theory problem. In the Supplementary Report of the Democratic members of the Joint Committee of March, 1955, one reads the following: "A sound and consistent position for the Council must be agreed upon; either it acts solely as an anonymous professional body advising the President or as the spokesmen before Congress and the public for the President's economic analyses and programs. If the first alternative is adopted, then some other spokesman for the President's overall economic position must be established."

The Council under the Eisenhower Administration has not taken a clearly consistent position on this issue. The chairman has made public speeches but has not freely appeared before the congressional committees, though he has appeared in executive sessions before the Joint Committee.

In my view, the Council should, strictly as technicians and not as political advocates, interpret the President's program before the public (preferably on rare occasions) and before congressional committees as requested. The position of the Council in this respect would be no different, I feel, from that of economists in the Federal Reserve Board (to take but one example) who have always been made available to explain Federal Reserve policy to congressional committees and to the public. There is no good reason why the Council of Economic Advisers may not act similarly as technical economists. This need in no way involve making political speeches or becoming political advocates. Senator Watkins, in his 1955 Supplementary Statement, has put it, I think, very well. The Council, he said, is a staff agency "advisory to a responsible official, but without operating responsibilities of its own." The Council members are indeed political appointees, but this does not imply "that they be something more than economists." They should not be employed in "the role of policy spokesmen," else they tend to "lose that objectiveness which is so essential to a staff agency." The Council members are economists, and they should not attempt to be something more than economists.

As the Latin proverb has it, *Tot homines quot sententiae.*

In the present context this might perhaps be paraphrased as follows: "There are as many economic opinions worthy of consideration as there are competent economists." "Pure economics" is scarcely better (perhaps worse) than "pure politics." If I read the record of economic progress correctly, time and again, it is the push of "pressure groups" which has led to the invention and installation of many, if indeed not most, of the institutional reforms which we now count as bulwarks of strength in the modern economy. Time and again professional economists have argued that the thing could not be done, and, if tried, would wreck the economy. The economist is not always a good leader, but he is essential as a technician in the innovation process. Yet not infrequently his marching orders must stem from political forces. New institutions are typically hammered out in the heat of political controversies. But competent economic guidance must play an important role in the evaluation of goals and in the implementation of workable new institutional arrangements.

The Employment Act of 1946 states specifically that it shall be the duty and function of the Council to assist and advise the President. It should not attempt the role of an independent entity operating on its own, ambitiously instructing the American people and the Congress with respect to its conception of "economic truth." It should not be a political arm of the party in power. Its function is clearly to assume the more humble role of adviser to the President and of technical interpreter of the President's program.

In conclusion, I wish to say that I regard the Employment Act of 1946 as a great Magna Carta of government planning for full employment.

CHAPTER 6

THE EMPLOYMENT ACT OF 1946 UNDER TRUMAN

A. Introduction

In this and the following chapter I propose to canvass and assess not so much the actual achievements of the economy during the past ten years but rather the policies which were proposed and, in retrospect, the wisdom of these policies. How has the machinery set up under the Employment Act of 1946 operated in practice?

I propose in particular to examine the Economic Reports of the President (and to some extent the Reviews issued by his Council of Economic Advisers) and also the recommendations of the Joint Committee (of the Congress) on the Economic Report. This running account, as one looks back with the wisdom of hindsight, will more or less automatically (without much help from me) constitute a critique of the policy recommendations. I shall consider the more significant Reports, moving back and forth from those of the President to those of the Joint Economic Committee.

The first Report of the President (January, 1947) is, I think, in retrospect, of greater significance than appeared evident at the time. It set up the analysis within the framework of the newly developed national accounting. It is easy for economists now to say, "Well, of course!" But it should not be overlooked that the Council might easily have been in hands which would have projected a quite different pattern of analysis. The first Report plumped firmly for the National Economic Budget and gave an excellent pedagogical discussion of concepts then relatively little known to the general informed public.

Next, the first Report plumped for the "cash budget" rather than the conventional budget—again a little-known concept and one that is destined, I believe, to play an increasingly significant role in our policy decisions.

The first Report set, moreover, an excellent precedent by (1) projecting goals for the coming year, and (2) recommending a division into (*a*) short-range programs and (*b*) long-range programs. All these are significant foundation stones laid in the formative years.

B. *The Problem of Inflation*

The 1948 Reports and the January, 1949, Report had as the central theme the problem of inflation. Wholesale prices, in fact, reached a turning point in January, 1948, declined throughout the first quarter, rose to a new peak in August, then fell rather abruptly through the rest of the year (due entirely to a drastic decline in the prices of farm products and foods) and stood, by January, 1949, 3 or 4 per cent below the January, 1948, level.

This price development, evident now as we look back, was, however, far from clear to current observers. People were still carrying around in their minds the memory of the sharp price increase of 1946 and 1947. Looking back, it is clear that the inflation had largely spent its force in the last quarter of 1947 and that the sharp January, 1948, decline in agricultural prices signaled the end of the postwar inflation. Two and one-half years later, just before the Korean crisis struck, wholesale prices stood indeed 6 per cent below the January, 1948, level. But in the January, 1948, Report much concern was expressed over the danger of the boom getting out of hand and possibly producing a bust, not altogether unlike the situation we were in in the summer of 1956.

On April 2, 1948, the Republican Congress passed a bill cutting taxes by some $5 billion just in the midst of this period of alleged inflation. This Act applied to the 1948 income. However, the first half of the 1948 tax revenues were derived largely from the income earned in 1947, which was taxed at the old rate. This higher tax rate produced a large Treasury surplus. The prospect, however, was dim for the tax receipts of the second half of 1948. This was due to three important budgetary developments: (1) a $3.5 billion increase in defense expenditures, (2) foreign aid, and (3) the Republican tax cut which applied to the 1948 income. And the July, 1948, Report bemoaned the tax cut "at a time when inflationary forces are still present."

Thus it was that the President, in the 1948 Midyear Report, called for a whole battery of defenses against inflation. This included a new excess-profits tax, consumer-credit and rent controls, increased power for the Federal Reserve, authority to regulate speculation in commodity exchanges, authority for control of allocation of scarce materials, inventory control, stand-by authority to ration products in short supply and to control the prices of scarce commodities.

The broad setup of powers which the President asked for is a measure of the concern over inflation. Still the Council of Economic Advisers at any rate was by no means sure which way the economy was going. In its July, 1948, Report [1] it pointed to certain counterinflationary factors, including the recent emergence of agricultural surpluses, the approximate

[1] A separate Review by the Council itself, much longer than the President's Report, was initiated in July, 1948. This involved much duplication, both with respect to recommendations and even with respect to factual materials, though the latter was extended in the Council's Review.

end of war-created shortages, and the prospect of large increases in output due to three years of vast investment in new plant and equipment. The Council noted the tremor of fear and uncertainty felt by the business community at the break of commodity prices early in 1948. Still, on balance the Council concluded that it would be a most dangerous error to assume that inflation had disappeared.

Enter now the famous Eightieth Congress, and the Joint Committee on the Economic Report, composed of seven senators and seven representatives. After a year of inactivity it had at last assembled a staff and by 1948 was prepared to report. The Republicans, headed by Senator Taft and Jesse Wolcott, were in control. The Committee Report was a scathing document. Complaint was made that the President's Report went far beyond the principal purpose of the Employment Act, namely, to maintain full employment and to avoid recurring depressions. Reaching far beyond this more limited objective, the President's Report encompassed a whole range of domestic policies—social welfare, health, education, natural resources, etc. All of this might indeed belong in the State of the Union message, but it had no place, it was averred, in the Economic Report.

The Joint Committee Report was emphatically opposed to granting the President authority to impose new controls; it was opposed to the President's $40 tax credit designed to relieve the burden of rising living costs for the low-income group; it alleged that taxes had reached the dangerously high figure of 25 per cent of Gross National Product, or 28 per cent [2] of the national income; it opposed the suggestion that serious deficiencies called for an increase in outlays on Federal public works from 2.0 in fiscal 1948 to 2.8 in fiscal 1949. The Committee Report asserted that a free economy must adapt

[2] Colin Clark had struck a popular chord with the business community when he asserted that 25 per cent represented an upper limit.

itself to changing conditions through appropriate adjustments of prices, costs, and production. Such adjustments, it alleged, are interfered with by rigid wages and rigid farm-price supports. The Report opposed the controls asked for by the President and called instead for more reliance on monetary policy.

But the Democrats on the Committee also had their inning. They issued a Minority Report. For the most part they supported, as might be expected, the President. They charged the majority in control of Congress with a policy of inaction, drift, and "trust to luck." They complained that this policy of inaction had depressed the purchasing power of the low-income group, and that this situation threatened the emergence of inadequate markets and depression. The minority urged three measures as follows: (1) Inflation should be stopped, (2) profits should be reduced by a new excess-profits tax as suggested by the President, and (3) a program to increase steel capacity.

By the time the President's 1949 Report was issued the August, 1948, break in prices (following the January, 1948, break) had already occurred. Reference was again made, as in an earlier Report, to the concern caused by the sharp break in prices in January, 1948. It was now emphatically stated—the Democrats had just won a victory at the polls—that the reason why this break had not led to collapse, as had been feared, was not just that we were luckier in 1948 than in 1929. Affirmative national policies had made the economy more shock-resistant. This included the farm-price-support program, social security, and the greatly strengthened financial and banking structure.

The system had withstood collapse, but inflation, it was alleged, was still a great danger. This, mind you, was in January, 1949, a year after the uptrend of prices had been stopped. The large cash surpluses of fiscal 1947 and 1948 had moderated the inflation, but had not, it was argued, been sufficient to terminate the inflationary trend—a trend augmented by the defense program and the 1948 tax reduction. On the other side, the escape from a general recession in 1948 did not mean, it was averred, that further dangers might not appear. We had been granted a breathing spell. But lasting prosperity awaited further effort and vigilance. We needed to have available a range of governmental measures which could be applied as brake or as accelerator according to need. The prevailing situation, the Report said, had mixed elements. The government needed both anti-inflationary and anti-deflationary escapes so that it could be ready for either contingency.

The Report noted that the postwar prosperity had rested in large part on temporary factors. The "momentum of war-created demand and war-created purchasing power has waned, and we must now rely more fully on currently generated purchasing power." But leaders in our enterprise economy should draw sustaining confidence from the fact that "it is the policy of the government under the Employment Act of 1946 to use all of its resources to avoid depression and to maintain continuous prosperity."

Jobs needed to be found for nearly one million net addition annually to the labor force. Output should gain by 3 to 4 per cent a year. Long-run expansionist policies should involve resource development, housing, health, and education. This involved, among other things, one million low-cost housing units spread over a seven-year period, urban redevelopment, Federal aid to elementary and secondary education, Federal scholarship for higher education, a national health-insurance program, Federal grants in support of hospital construction and aid to educate more doctors, dentists, and nurses, and, finally, an expansion of social security.

These long-range programs, it was noted, had to be reconciled with short-run policies designed to curb inflation. The minimum requirements of the more essential programs—inter-

national reconstruction, resource development, and social welfare—might require the temporary exercise of selective controls. We "do not want to sacrifice that security and welfare
because of narrow and selfish concepts as to the acceptable
limits of government action." We would rather have those
"relatively unpleasant restrictions on our freedom of action
for a while than imperil our security or allow our human and
material resources to deteriorate."

Thus by January, 1949, the President had gone beyond the
stage of merely fighting inflation. Inflation was still a concern.
But there was also the fear that, in the absence of an expansionist program (to take the place of the temporary factors
causing the postwar boom), depression might come. And anyway the long-run programs were pressing. They could no
longer wisely be postponed. Even in the face of some remaining inflationary pressures they must still be undertaken. However, in view of the inflationary pressures, increased expenditures called for additional taxes. The President asked for $4
billion more taxes, the principal source being a tax on corporate profits and some increase in the individual tax rate in
upper and middle brackets. Social-insurance contributions
should be increased according to schedule. The increased
reserve requirements, expiring June 30, 1949, should be extended and should apply to all insured banks; and the consumer
installment credit regulations expiring in June 30, 1949, should
be extended. Both of these had been granted in the special
session called by the President in the midst of the 1948 election.
Mandatory allocation controls on key materials in short supply
should be authorized together with selective price and wage
controls. Thus the President once again went all out in his
1949 Report [3] for an extensive increase in his powers to fight
both inflation and deflation.

[3] The Council's 1949 Review elaborated the President's Report, especially on the matter of basic programs for balanced growth. Nearly 30
pages were devoted to this subject.

The new Congress was Democratic. Senator O'Mahoney was chairman of the Joint Committee when its 1949 Report came in, and Dr. Theodore Krebs, of Stanford, was the economic consultant.

The President had presented a big program involving greatly extended powers. The Democratic members of the Joint Committee noted that it is only in the economic field that objection to planning is raised. The Democrats supported the President's request for a $4 billion increase in taxes. It urged that the most rigid economy be observed by the government in order to balance the budget and establish a surplus. Deficit financing, said the Joint Committee Report, might be necessary in depression, but in times of prosperity taxes should be high enough to reduce the debt. The Democrats noted that if the whole $4 billion tax increase asked for came from corporations, profits after taxes would still be as high as in 1947. The Democratic majority noted that the Federal government's fiscal operations during 1948 (when the Republicans controlled Congress), far from helping to control inflation, had been the "main expansionary force in the economy." [4] The $5 billion tax reduction, Foreign Aid Assistance Act, and the increased defense outlays were the "main factors ending the economic hesitancy of the first quarter of 1948 and initiating the renewed rise in business activity and prices."

On the face of it the Democratic majority thus seemed to approve the Republicans' tax reductions of 1948. Their Report is dated February 21, 1949. Prices were falling, and this may in

[4] Was 1948 a year of overemployment? Note the following question (p. 29) in the Report: "If 1948 be considered a superboom year of overemployment, what level of National Income should this committee set for itself in discharging its obligations under the Employment Act of 1946? Should it be as much as 20 per cent below 1948 or no more than 5 per cent?"

Actually in the following years, 1951 to 1953, unemployment declined relative to 1948, output increased enormously, and prices were stable. In retrospect the questions raised take on a different hue.

part account for the fact that the Committee members evidenced less worry than had the President over inflation. They noted that, except for automobiles, there was no longer any consumer item in short supply. Business witnesses before the Joint Committee had opposed the President's request for selective price controls and higher taxes on the ground that prices had already leveled off.

The Democratic majority nevertheless supported stand-by authority to fix cooling-off periods before price increases, such as steel, could be put into effect by business corporations. Also the Democratic majority supported the President's request for credit control and for selective price controls.

Senator Taft had asked the round table of experts who appeared before the Joint Committee what could now replace the war-created backlog of consumer and capital expenditures which had kept the economy going thus far. The Democratic members had an answer. They urged that a higher consumption pattern was needed.

They expressed grave doubts that the ratio of total investment to Gross National Product could long remain as high as it had been in 1948. The ratio of consumption to GNP should be raised. They pointed out that business was still preparing to weather a recurrence of "boom and bust." Dare the individual company, asked the Democratic members, bank on the sustained high levels of prosperity envisaged in the Employment Act? Is it safe for business to gamble on the maintenance of a steady and high level of activity? If not, then the break-even point must be at a low-output level. This means a wage-cost-price relationship which ensures exceptionally large profits at full employment. But these profits mean a lack of balance between investment and consumption. High prosperity profits are indeed needed if they are to be followed by depression losses. Yet these profits undermine the high-output, high-wage, low-profit-margin economy needed to sustain high-level employment.

In a sustained full-employment economy the ratio of consumption to national income must be higher than it is in a boom-and-bust economy at the peak of prosperity. The relationship of 1920 and 1929 proved to be highly unstable. The fact that the relationship of 1948 was approximately similar to that of 1920 and 1919 was consequently not reassuring.

Yet no businessman dares to raise his break-even point unless he can be assured against depression. Without any demonstrated experience showing that the laudable aims of the Employment Act of 1946 can, in fact, be consistently achieved, the individual business firms, no matter how large, cannot afford to risk insolvency. This, said the Democrats, is the dilemma that confronts us.[5]

The Republican minority issued its own report. It rejected the basic philosophy of the President's Report. In the view of the Republican members the President's Report recommended in effect a planned and controlled economy with increased taxation. It carried on a crusade for more Executive power. It ignored, so said the Republicans, the indirect approach through monetary and fiscal policy.

The President's Reports threaten, it was alleged, to become "political propaganda rather than scientific analysis." The Republican members saw no reason why the Economic Report "should not state the arguments on both sides where the economic issues are inextricably involved in politics." The Report should be devoted primarily to solving the problem of full and continuous employment and should not be diverted too much by social political issues.

[5] See in this connection pp. 254–256 of my *Economic Policy and Full Employment*, 1947, from which the Committee's statement on the break-even point appears to be largely derived.

The Republicans stressed the monetary and fiscal weapons to prevent depressions, but even these weapons should be used cautiously and only when dangerous trends have already developed. The Republican members believed that the Economy had already by 1948 very largely adjusted itself to a new balanced situation. Profits and investment, they conceded, were perhaps a little high, but they could be expected rapidly to adjust as a buyers' market began to take over in place of the hitherto-prevailing sellers' market.

The Republicans expressed the belief that the greatest threat to the stability of the economy lay in the constantly increasing burden of taxation and in the difficulty of securing sufficient capital formation for growth. Their minority Report recommended reduction in government expenditures, anticyclical use of public works, credit control by the Federal Reserve, no selective controls at present, antimonopoly measures, farm-price supports, and a housing program.

The Republicans objected to the frequent use in the President's Report of generalities and question-begging words such as "proper," "wise," "needed," "adequate," "salutary," etc. The programs suggested seemed to them to presuppose easy answers.

Very important differences of opinion related to inflation and distortions in the economy. Inflation was a major concern in the President's Report. The Republican members, however, questioned the danger of inflation. The President's Report had had much to say about the distortions caused by the price increases of 1946–1947. The Republicans expressed doubt that any serious distortions were evident. They expressed their belief (a belief which I regard as sound) that the economy was, in fact, well balanced, with no serious distortions and no serious danger of either inflation or deflation. They expressed doubt that the economic advisers of the President were really confident of their own grounds. The situation had been called "mixed." The economy, so it would appear, according to the Council, was going in two directions at once.

The Republicans made the interesting point that the Council had, in fact, as experience showed, often set its sights too low. In the 1947 Report they had suggested an employment goal only slightly above that of 1946. A year later employment stood 2½ million over 1946. Again in 1948 the Council set the goal at the 1947 level, but in January, 1949, employment had increased by over 1 million. The economy outperformed the goals set.

The Republican minority felt unhappy about developments under the Employment Act. When the Joint Committee was established "it was the hope of many that it would approach its task from a completely scientific and nonpartisan position, relying on expert economic advisers"; that it would not become "a piece of machinery representing those temporarily in control of Congress, and functioning only to approve and praise the Economic Report of the President." The use of the Joint Committee Report as a "political forum by an uncritical majority threatens the long-run usefulness of the Joint Committee, and of the Employment Act itself. This is the background which has prompted us to file a minority report."

C. The Recession Reports

By the time the Midyear Report of 1949 was issued it was obvious to everyone that the country was experiencing a recession. The January, 1949, Report had indeed evidenced some uneasiness, but that we were on the edge of a recession was not then fully realized.

The Midyear Report took much pride in the moderateness of this decline. Credit was given to the built-in stabilizers and to the increased cash payments of the government, which ran 20 per cent higher in the first half of 1949 than in the first half

of 1948, to the housing program, and to the government credit
agencies. The Report still had much to say about "distortions
in the price system," but no evidence of this was presented.
The inflation (which, it was alleged, Congress, not following
the President's recommendations, had failed to stop), together
with the distortions it had created, was blamed for the recession. Downward price adjustments, but not wage cuts, were
recommended as means to increase employment.

Later, in a somewhat contradictory section, it was stated
that the decline had been moderate because no cumulative
collapse had been set going by serious distortions in the system.
There had been no speculative spree, no excess inventory
accumulations, and no excessive increases in personal indebted-
ness.

Unemployment had reached 3.9 million, or 6 per cent of the
labor force. The price decline (9 per cent) was called moderate.[6] Profits were down 13 per cent, and farm income was
down 8 per cent.

The Report stressed the need not merely to prevent depression but to work toward expansion. Essential national programs—security, development, and welfare—must not be cut
back.

This position posed a quandary for the President, but only
because he did not face the issue squarely. How reconcile these
expenditure programs with budgetary policy? In previous Reports he had been stressing the danger of inflation. He had
sharply criticized the Republican tax of 1948. Now that recession was upon us he should unequivocally have invoked a
compensatory fiscal policy. Instead, the issue was hedged with
weasel words. On the one side it was quite rightly argued that
the debt-reduction objective cannot be blindly pursued irre-

[6] Professional economists almost always have a bias toward deflation.
A 9 per cent price decline in one year is regarded as moderate; a 9 per
cent increase in one year is regarded as highly dangerous.

spective of the state of the economy. National taxes, the President said, should be flexible. But he stated this principle in overly simplified terms, as, in fact, is far too often done by timid economists. His simple rule was that taxes should be raised in good times [7] and lowered in depression. This simple rule of course condemned the Republican tax cut of 1948. In fact, however, this tax cut was thoroughly justified by subsequent events. It produced no inflation, and it certainly minimized the recession of 1949. But even the simple rule was not followed by the President himself. The country was in a recession. Yet, contrary to his own principle, he did not recommend a tax cut.

The pious hope was expressed that an expanding economy would eventually bring a balanced budget. It was not recognized that an increase in public credit, no less than private credit, might well be necessary to produce an expanding economy.

Compensatory and long-range fiscal policy was not discussed frankly and scientifically on an adult, sophisticated plane. A note of apology was struck—a confession of a temporary lapse from virtue! Greater evils were to be avoided by committing a small sin—so the argument seemed to run. Economic and social deficits were labeled "far more serious than a temporary deficit in the Federal budget."

Now this is not the way to discuss the merits or demerits of a compensatory fiscal policy. Popular prejudices are nurtured and folklore misunderstandings are deepened by hopes (which may well be illusory) that if we "pursue an expansionist fiscal policy, we will not only be able to balance the budget but we can resume debt reduction." This, I fear, verges on double talk.

While all-out emergency measures were not advocated in

[7] Taxes should not be raised in good times unless necessary to prevent price inflation. Raising taxes might kill the good times and bring on recession.

the President's Report, the recession, it was argued, did call for some action. The recommendations include liberalization of unemployment benefits together with a Federal reinsurance fund, extension of veterans' unemployment benefits for another year, liberalization of old-age insurance, and an increase of Federal public works from $2½ billion to $3 billion.[8]

The recession was far from over when the President's January, 1950, Report was issued. Indeed, as events unfolded, the peak of the unemployment was reached in February, 1950,

[8] The Council's Review interpreted the recession as a "liquidation of inflation without being overcome by business depression." In the early postwar years, factors favorable to employment included the backlog of demands, liquid savings, and a large Federal budget for defense and international aid. As these temporary supports slackened, continued prosperity, it was argued, would require a wide range of adjustments.

Earlier Council Reviews had warned again and again that inflation would create distortions that would eventually lead into depression. Drastic action had, time and again, been urged upon Congress by the President, but, as we have seen, Congress largely ignored the recommendations. Still the Council in its own Review (July, 1948) stated that the actions taken were sufficient to "prevent a very substantial degree of inflation from developing," and that it had been effective enough "to prevent the kind of exaggerated speculative spree which could end only in a disastrous slump." The inflationary tendency eased off gradually, until eventually the pressures disappeared "without being followed by a collapse of the price structure."

The Council credited (as had the President) the moderateness of the recession to the built-in stabilizers, the increased outlays in public works, defense and foreign aid, deposit insurance, and low private debt. No credit is given to the Republican tax cut. The belief is expressed that "we may have the unique and fortunate experience of liquidating a major inflation without falling into a severe recession."

Wage cutting was frowned upon, but downward price adjustments were recommended. Slashing government expenditures would only aggravate deflationary trends. Tax increases should be avoided. A deficit would have to be accepted. Thus the old prescriptions of the twenties were indeed laid to rest, but very little positive action was recommended. The Council Review, it will be noted, was essentially a restatement of the President's Report.

with 4.7 million unemployed, or 7.6 per cent of the civilian labor force. That was in a Democratic Administration. Imagine the furore which Democratic senators would have stirred up had unemployment reached 7.6 per cent in a Republican Administration.

When we have a Republican President, the opposition party is busy every minute of the day pushing the Administration into action, and the whole country becomes very sensitive to even a little unemployment. When we have a Democratic President, the opposition party is busy every minute of the day trying hard to keep the Administration from "rocking the boat." Thus it is not altogether impossible that we enjoy the best of two worlds when we have a Republican President scared to death of another Hoover depression and a Democratic congress egging him on to action.

The 1950 Report suggested that an "adjustment period" was inevitable before we could reach a firm basis for stability and steady economic growth. However, this "relatively safe passage from inflation to greater stability was no accident." Government measures, it was said, cushioned the downswing and lent strong support to recovery.

The President placed the blame for the recession upon Congress. "In earlier economic reports I emphasized the dangers of permitting inflationary pressures to continue, and urged measures to hold them in check. Most of these measures were not adopted, and the break in the economic boom, against which I had warned, came to pass."

The areas enjoying expansion throughout the recession were automobiles and public and private construction, especially residential construction. Government cash payments (social security, farm-price supports, defense and foreign-aid programs) increased.

The goals set forth in the Report included the following: Unemployment should be reduced to 2 million or at most 2½ million; productivity per worker should rise 2 or 2½ per cent a year; resource development, education, health, and social security should be regarded as essential programs in the Federal budget; over the years the budget should be balanced, with some surplus for debt reduction; wage increases should be related to productivity; adjustments should be made in prices and incomes which would translate potential markets into real markets.

The President again bemoaned the untimely reduction in taxes in 1948. As business improves we should provide, he said, some surplus for debt reduction. Movement in this direction should be accelerated by moderate increases in tax rates. But there should be no cut in expenditures—indeed the essential Federal programs should be expanded.

Regret was expressed over the termination (June 30, 1949) of the Federal Reserve authority to control installment credit, which action had led, the Report said, to excessive relaxation in consumer credit. Farm-price support should be shifted to income payments.

The Council's 1950 Review declared that the year 1949 had demonstrated "our improved capacity to protect the economy against depressions growing out of moderate recessions, and to fortify those forces to which a free economy must look for renewed expansion." [9]

The Council found the prospects for 1950 encouraging. Among these were: (1) The large payment of insurance dividends to veterans to be made the first half of 1950. (This, in fact, raised transfer payments from $11.9 billion rate in 1948 to

[9] Blame for the decline in 1949 was placed upon the failure of demand to grow in proportion to the increasing potential output. Rising prices, it was alleged, "limited the growth of demand."

Rising costs are indeed often a factor leading to reduced investment at the end of a boom. The "buyers' strike" argument may at times have a very limited validity. All in all, however, the Reports elsewhere give far better reasons why the 1948 boom ended.

$20.6—annual rate—in the first quarter of 1950.) (2) The "great potential demand of business and consumers supported by ample funds and credit." (3) The prospects for residential construction.

A large section was devoted to economic growth. Growth objectives were set out for a five-year period, 1950 to 1954. "Balanced" relationships of consumption, investment, and government outlays were projected. As a matter of interest I present, corrected for price changes, the following table, which compares the Council's median projections with the actual figures for 1954 in billions of dollars.

	Council median projection (billions)	Actual figure reached (billions)
Gross National Product	$343	$357
Consumption	247	234
Private investment	46	46
Government outlays	50	77

As the table shows, the projection for government outlays was understandably too low, and this cut down severely the consumption figure. But the GNP actually reached exceeded considerably the Council's expectations.

In this Report (1950)—the first one under the chairmanship of Keyserling—the Council shifted ground with respect to price policy. Under Nourse the Council had always had a predilection for downward price adjustments. Now the Council definitely proclaimed preference for upward adjustments of money incomes to correspond with productivity increases. The 1950 Report stated that a fairly stable price level is more conducive to business confidence than a generally declining price level. It was recognized that divergent growth in productivity in different industries must produce divergent relative prices between different goods and services. Industries with exceptionally large increases in productivity can make downward price adjustments.[10]

The Council noted that it had not, in its July, 1949, Report urged increases in Federal spending "for the purpose of stimulating the economy." It had, in fact, urged increases on general grounds of growth needs. The Council stressed its "confidence in the internal recuperative forces which thus far has been justified." This, it seems to me, appears a great deal like carrying water on both shoulders. Or perhaps worse yet, it sounds as if the Council were a bit apologetic for having recommended what in fact amounted to a compensatory spending program.

The Council favored neither tax cuts nor large tax increases. The tax cut of 1948 was still regarded as unfortunate. But since the Economy had by now adjusted itself to the lower rates, the Council now favored only moderate rate increases. The national debt, it was argued, should be reduced.

The Joint Committee Report, with Democrats in control, was conciliatory toward its own minority members. It stressed a range of things that both parties could in the main agree upon. It agreed with the President that essential Federal programs must be supported in order to promote a sound, advancing economy. The problems of the low-income groups were again stressed. The President's proposals were summarized and somewhat cautiously supported. The Democratic members were not convinced that new directives should be issued with respect to the division of authority between the Federal Reserve and the Treasury, nor that new instructions were in order with respect to the objectives of monetary and debt-management policies. Further study of this important

[10] See my *Economic Policy and Full Employment*, 1947, pp. 241–243, where the arguments favoring this policy had been fully elaborated.

problem was urged. Senator Douglas felt disappointed over this position and wrote a brief supplementary report.

The Republican minority issued a brief report of about ten pages. It recalled its strong dissent from the basic philosophy of the Economic Report of 1949. Congress had refused to go along, and events had proved, so argued the minority, that Congress was right. If conditions are currently as satisfactory as the 1950 Economic Report says, it could not, they said, be on account of the President's recommendations, because these were for the most part rejected by Congress.

Again the Republican minority made the objection that the Economic Report was primarily a political document demanding ever more power for the President. The Republican members called the Report diffuse and hortatory. The President's Report (so said the minority) proclaimed the philosophy of high spending, public medicine, Brannan plan, public power, etc. The budget was to be balanced, they noted, not by curtailing spending but from a growth in the GNP to be achieved through still further spending. They rejected this idea. The Republicans expressed the belief that the President's program would stifle growth.

The Republican minority cited six important measures urged by the President in January, 1949, which were turned down by Congress, including the request for a $4 billion increase in taxes, the authority to employ various price and allocation controls, authority to expand steel capacity, and expenditures on education and health. The minority group asserted that it was the restraint and judgment displayed by Congress which had restored business confidence.

The Republicans found the argument in the Economic Report "smooth" and "clever" but containing no economic analysis or sustainable logic. The problems can't be solved, they said, by mere exhortation. The easy declarations of the government that full employment will be maintained had yet to be tested. The postwar backlogs of demand, it was averred, had so far postponed that day of reckoning.

The country was confronted, said the Republicans, with two conflicting views. One is the planned economy with mandatory allocations and selective controls. The other is the broad approach based on monetary and debt-management policies, and the maintenance of competition. The monetary tools had been thrown away—spiked by deliberate choice, flouted by the Administration in favor of its cheap-money policy. Government programs can't be increased indefinitely. Must deficits be accepted, it was asked, as the way of life?

The Republicans found that the Economic Report had no word on incentives. While the government "exhorts," taxes continue to be painful deterrents. The government has created uncertainty and has undermined confidence. Business and investors are in a continuous state of apprehension. The Republicans suggested that the President's Report should consider and promote the fundamental factors which encourage private investment rather than attempt "to plug the holes created by failure of government policies to foster private initiative and responsibility."

The Republicans referred to the loose fiscal policies of the government and the President's neat and easy way of disposing of deficits. All is to be cured by the "health of the economy"! This, the Republicans declared, is indeed an amazing statement. The probable cost of fifteen of the President's proposals would be $7 billion now and eventually $25 billion annually. We are urged to spend money (said the Report) to create greater deficits, to generate greater income, and finally to wipe out the deficits created through the programs! The Republicans strongly dissented.

Had some clairvoyant undertaken to disclose to the Republican members the increases in the Federal budget which would in fact occur in 1951–1953, the expansion both in private consumption and investment, the prodigious increase in output —all this with price stability and less than 2 million unemployed—it is not difficult to imagine the skepticism with which his forecast would have been received.

D. The Korean Crisis

How these controversies might have ended, and what would have been the course of employment and production, had no Korean crisis broken out, no one will ever know. Out of the Korean experience a vast deal was learned, controversies over economic policies were softened, the economic climate was changed. The return of the Republicans to power in 1953 hastened and consolidated this *rapprochement*. But we are running ahead of our story. There was still much water to flow over the dam.

By the time the Midyear Report of 1950 was published the Korean crisis was upon us. All bets were off. It is easier to agree to curtail inflationary pressures caused by a *forced* expansion than to agree upon debatable programs for full employment voluntarily arrived at.

The Midyear Report stated that the prodigious installations of new plant and machinery during the past five years were at long last beginning to show fruits.[11] Productivity per man-hour was rising 3 per cent per year. The President again struck out at limited steel capacity and urged that expansion of capacity of basic industries should not be held back by fears of depression.

The President renewed his requests (now far more urgent) for authority to regulate consumer and real-estate credit, and for priorities and allocation controls. He appealed for a sharp increase in corporation and individual income taxes.

[11] The Council, in its Midyear Review, presented a survey of Five Years of Postwar Economic Developments.

In the January, 1951, Economic Report, the President regretted that the needed expansion in welfare programs could not be made in view of the Korean War. Federal aid to education was, however, being extended to school districts overburdened as a result of Federal military activities.

In view of the inflationary impact of the vast military budget we should make it a first principle, the Report urged, to pay the cost of national defense on a pay-as-you-go basis. The President complimented Congress on the successful enactment of two important tax measures. In view of the growing budget, additional taxes must be levied. Both corporations and individuals must pay much higher taxes. Excise taxes should also be increased. In February, 1951, and again in July, the President asked for another $10 billion increase in taxes over and above the two tax measures already passed.

In the January, 1952, Report the President was able to report that three major tax bills had been enacted during the preceding eighteen months. Again the President urged additional tax legislation.

In its July, 1952, Review the Council presented an extensive appraisal of the postwar period with special reference to the stabilizers built into our system and how they had worked. Attention was then turned to the problems ahead when security spending would stop rising and perhaps decline. There was discussion of long-range private investment, of tax reduction, of housing and urban redevelopment, and of the strong measures the government was prepared to take to prevent depression.

And now to catch up on the Report of the Joint Committee. The 1951 Report came rather late—on March 26, 1951. It recognized the need of pay-as-you-go financing in order to stop inflation. It agreed that it was within our power to achieve the output goals set up by the President—a 7 per cent increase in output in 1951, and 28 per cent in the next five years. (The actual increase, as it turned out, was 6.8 per cent in 1951 and 22.4 per cent over the five years 1950 to 1955.)

The alert Committee had unanimously recommended as early as July 21, 1950, an immediate increase in taxes, restriction on consumer credit, and contraction of housing loans. The Defense Production Act of 1950 granted authority to fix ceilings on prices and wages. The Korean crisis found the Joint Committee more alert than the President and the Council. The Committee heartily welcomed the famous accord of March, 1951, between the Federal Reserve and the Treasury.

Supplementary views were presented by the Republicans— Watkins, Wolcott, and Herter. They noted with pleasure the marked shift in emphasis in the President's 1951 Report compared with previous Reports with respect to nonmilitary government spending programs and financial limitations. In the 1950 Minority Report warnings had been issued about the then prevailing spending and lending policies which it was charged were inevitably carrying the nation toward inflation and financial chaos. The President's 1951 Report at long last recognizes "the thin margin of safety left in our economic structure as a result of unsound (and too-long continued) fiscal, monetary, and other questionable economic policies." (They apparently forgot that in the 1950 Minority Report they had argued that the economy was nicely in balance with no serious distortions.)

Chairman O'Mahoney, for the Democrats, acknowledged the cooperative spirit of the minority members but denied any shift in emphasis. Fighting inflation in wartime, he said, required different policies from fighting deflation.

In the Joint Committee Report of February 25, 1952, the Democratic majority suggested that possibly there was indeed some upper limit to taxes (though not an inflexible per cent *à la* Colin Clark) beyond which further tax increases would aggravate and reduce initiative and output. There was much evidence, however, that the United States had not yet reached that limit. The Majority Report recommended tightening the loopholes but wanted no further increase in rates. This position was taken because the Democratic members believed that the cash deficit could be held to an amount where its inflationary impact could be controlled by other programs. The Democrats therefore opposed the President's request for further tax increases.

Two Democratic senators, Douglas and Benton, believed that the President and the Council were too complacent about the prospective deficit and the possibility of relying on controls to stop inflation. Congress would have to adopt heroic measures if we were to save the country from inflation. The Joint Committee Report should, moreover, be more specific, they thought, about the control of bank credit. If expenses could be cut by $7.6 million and revenues increased by $2.4 million, a balanced cash budget could be achieved.

The Minority Report, including all the Republicans, again complained that the President's 1952 Report consisted of high-sounding words but lacked conviction. The Republican group noted that the Democrats on the Committee rejected the President's high-spending proposals and his request for an increase in taxes. The Republicans complained that the Democratic majority had failed to recognize adequately the importance of monetary and credit policy. They expressed the belief that much of the restraint imposed by the new taxes had been dissipated by the delay in freeing the Federal Reserve from Treasury domination. The Republicans stood firmly for three things: (1) reduction in expenditures, (2) no increase in taxes, and (3) a firm and independent Federal Reserve to control money and credit.

E. The Democrats' Swan Song

The 1953 Report closed the books for the Democrats. No special interest could possibly attach to the President's statement. The Council Review is essentially an academic document. It is a carefully integrated product, for which a highly competent staff is to be congratulated no less than the Council itself. Special credit is given to the staff economists in this Report.

The Council's Review begins with an excellent summary of developments in 1952 (including a large number of very useful charts), together with a chapter on near-term prospect and policies. But the bulk of the report relates to methodology. How best can the purposes of the Employment Act be served by the Economic Reports? This is the basic question raised. The discussion is important and illuminating.

It is argued that it is neither practical nor necessary, for purposes of effective action, to forecast precisely the exact time when the economic climate will change. The short run will seem less important if we work *constantly* toward the maintenance of maximum production and employment. We may properly concern ourselves with the long run, because long-run policies are vital to the maintenance of a *currently* healthy economy.

The near-term outlook is largely determined by *forces which are already in being*, and therefore leaves *much room for forecasting* but relatively *little room for policy*. The long-run outlook, on the other hand, places little emphasis upon forecasting and more emphasis upon policy formation.

The Council expressed the belief that the attainment of the goal of the Employment Act depends not so much on accurate forecasting as on the popular commitment to the goal and the continuous pursuit of that goal by a day-to-day improvement of analysis and policy formation.

The Council noted the methodology set forth in the Employment Act, namely, (*a*) to identify employment and production goals, (*b*) to estimate prospective trends *in the event* that policies remain constant, and (*c*) to recommend changes in policies designed to bring the prospective trends in line with the goals.

Accordingly the Council believed it important to make projections based on estimates of needs and capabilities. As an illustration it made a projection of GNP for the years 1953–1955. It will be of interest to compare the projections with the figures that actually unfolded, corrected for price changes. They are as follows:

Year	Council projections of GNP (billions)	Actual figures for GNP (billions)
1953	$365	$365
1954	376	360
1955	388	387

The Council disclosed at some length the methodology involved in its sector-by-sector analysis.

1. An appraisal of where the economy is now. Is it moving currently under the momentum of a maintainable rate of prosperity, or is it trying to gain speed after a stall?

2. We start by assuming no change in current policies. If desired changes were postulated at the outset, we would be assuming at the start the results of the inquiry.

3. Exogenous changes (fortuitous events) are ruled out. Endogenous forces are presumed to predominate.

Estimates are then made of the prospective trend of GNP and its major component parts, assuming no changes in policy.

These prospective trends should then be compared with *projections* of GNP and its component parts based on such knowledge as we have of past *relationships* which may be regarded as *maintainable*. It is these long-run balanced relationships which we should strive for. The all-important relationships for sustainable growth are, of course, the ratios of investment to GNP and to consumption.

Involved here are not only economic decisions based on sustainable relationships considered from the standpoint of economic workability but also social decisions based on value judgments. With respect to the broad problem of social priorities, choices must be made, largely on noneconomic grounds, between public expenditures and private expenditures (e.g., schools versus automobiles). Next comes the problem of economic priorities—the optimum relation of investment and consumption. "There is a limit to how far either investment growth or consumption growth can outrun the other without pausing for the laggard to catch up" (p. 108).

This 1953 Council Review is a notable document and deserves more attention than has been given to it by professional economists.

CHAPTER 7

THE EMPLOYMENT ACT UNDER THE EISENHOWER ADMINISTRATION

A. Republican Support for the Employment Act

After twenty years, control of the government passed into the hands of the Republicans. The Employment Act barely weathered the storm. But once this hurdle was passed, the new Council quickly gained a position as a part of the governmental machinery. The course of events favored this development. No sooner was the new Administration installed than a recession began to threaten. The business world wanted assurance that the government would not let the economy down. The Administration gave them this assurance and in so doing leaned heavily upon the machinery set up under the Employment Act.

The main significance of the 1954 Economic Report [1] was the firm declaration by the President and his Administration that the government would use its "vast powers to help maintain employment and purchasing power," and that the government's responsibility is "not a start-and-stop responsibility, but a continuous one." This disposed once and for all of such

[1] Hereafter the midterm Report was abandoned. Only the January Report was required by the Act. Also it should be noted that it now became exclusively the Report of the President alone. The Council as such made no Economic Report, only a report on its activities.

views as (1) that the economy was henceforth going to be left to run on its own (a point of view feared, yet widely advocated by business) and (2) that the Employment Act related only to short-run cyclical problems (a view widely held by conservative supporters of the Act).

It is especially interesting to note how the Joint Committee, both the Republican majority and the Democratic minority, responded to the Economic Report of the New Administration. For the first time a unanimous Report (with supplementary statements by individual members) was issued by the Joint Committee. This was a notable event, in sharp contrast with the earlier sharply divided Reports on strictly party lines.

The opening paragraph of the Joint Committee Report refers to the passing of the Employment Act eight years ago by an overwhelming bipartisan vote. Instead of the usual partisan criticism the Report referred with approval to the government's efforts, under the Act, to dampen and limit the war-created inflationary pressures. It referred to the operations of the Act during the 1949–1950 recession and recovery. The Joint Committee noted with approval President Eisenhower's repeated expressions of belief in the basic principles of the Employment Act. The Committee commended the President and the new Council on the quality of the 1954 Economic Report. The Committee asserted that past Reports had always been useful, but found the statistical materials and the analysis contained in the 1954 Report "even more valuable than in the past." The Report was, the Committee thought, a distinct forward step in helping to make the Employment Act effective.

That the Democratic members could join in these statements is perhaps not too surprising. More surprising was the bipartisan expression of dissatisfaction with certain specific features of the Economic Report. The Committee believed that the Report could be much improved if the proposals were set forth in summary form rather than being diffused throughout the entire Report. Much more important was the criticism that the Report had not set out, as required by the Act, the levels of employment and production needed to assure full employment. The Committee proceeded in its own Report to supplement the Economic Report by developing through its hearings greater clarity in the trends needed to maintain maximum employment. Also, the staff materials attached to the Committee's Report suggested the nature and magnitude of the necessary adjustments.

B. *The Joint Committee Becomes Aggressive*

In reviewing and analyzing the President's 1954 Report, the Joint Economic Committee held more exhaustive hearings than in earlier years in order to get the "best available viewpoints on the economic outlook and the implications for Federal economic policy."

The Committee was unanimous in its belief that the Employment Act itself is a strong reason for viewing the years of transition optimistically. "If the government accepts its responsibility to create a climate and to pursue programs which will advance the objective of the Employment Act, we believe that complementary private demands for investment and consumption will be sufficient." The Committee agreed with the President that "the arsenal of weapons at the disposal of the government for maintaining economic stability is formidable." The Committee urged all-out preparations to "use these weapons as need arises."

The Committee went firmly on record that the economy was fully capable of "meeting safely additional military expenditures if such expenditures are necessary for our military security." Thus the Committee sharply contested the view of leading Administration officials who held that the economy "could not take it." Reductions in military expenditures should be made "upon their merits and not upon the premise that they are made necessary for economic reasons."

The Committee unanimously accepted the view that economic conditions might well deteriorate so that the Federal government may be called upon to act "promptly and vigorously," accepting a deficit as the most appropriate fiscal policy.

The Committee favored liberalization of the social-security system, agreed on school lunches and foreign relief as means of disposing of some farm surpluses. The Committee feared that the "proposals contained in the Economic Report may actually place the farm family in a worse position in the short run." (On the farm problem there were a number of individual statements from members of both parties.) The Committee argued that public-housing and slum-clearance programs can be important sustaining forces in the years ahead.

There was general agreement on international-trade policy. The Committee was somewhat disturbed over undue optimism expressed in the Economic Report about public-works preparedness. The Committee was particularly critical of the President's heavy reliance upon state and local communities without offer of substantial Federal aid. It was pointed out that most local communities are "bound by tax, debt, or user-charge limitations." It thus seemed clear to the Committee that "the Federal government's credit must be substantially relied upon." The Committee recommended proposals to facilitate the immediate planning and coordination, through an administrator directly responsible to the President, of all Federal public-works and community developments with the cooperation of the Federal, State, and local governments.

The Committee placed "fiscal policy high among the tools available to the government for dealing with the problem of economic stability and growth." The Committee commended and approved the principle set forth in the President's State of the Union message which expressly "recognizes that the Federal budget should be a stabilizing factor in the economy."

The Committee Report called attention to suggestions made in the hearings that accelerated depreciation might well be used as a countercyclical device. With respect to the so-called double taxation of dividends, the Committee suggested careful examination of the Administration's proposals to inquire whether they in fact make for the "greatest equity among individual taxpayers."

Clearly something had happened. The Joint Committee as a whole was in a new mood. Instead of much negative criticism there was unanimous support for a strong positive program. The President's proposals did not go far enough even for the Republican members. The Report was unanimous. This was indeed something new. Even the supplemental statement of five Democrats, which asked for more drastic action, stressed their general agreement with the Committee Report and warmly supported the "highly nonpartisan spirit" in which the hearings had been conducted and noted with genuine approval the degree of cooperation between the Committee, the chairman, and the staff. The 1954 Joint Committee Report clearly ushered in a new day for the Employment Act.

C. The President's 1955 Report

The President's Economic Report, 1955, renewed firmly the Eisenhower declaration that the "government will shoulder its full responsibility." The Report recognized (without reference to its New Deal origin) that "we have developed in our country a fiscal system that tends to cushion or offset a decline in private income." Tax reductions, along with social-securities payments, supported powerfully the income at the disposal of individuals and families in the 1954 recession.

The President's Report failed again, as did that of 1954, to stress the growing community needs and the necessary part which the Federal government must play if these needs are to be met. Instead it expressed the view that a "high and rising standard of living brings to more of our people the opportunity for continued intellectual and spiritual growth." But school and other community services do not automatically spring from higher pay envelopes. The problem of social priorities was not squarely faced.

D. The Forward Look of the Joint Committee

Again in 1955 the Joint Committee Report is of special interest. This time the Democrats controlled the Committee in a Republican Administration. In 1947–1948 it was the other way round—a Republican-controlled Committee in a Democratic Administration. But here the parallel stops. This time the Committee brought in a unanimous report.

The Joint Committee Report declared firmly for an expanding economy. "Because of our growing population and our spectacular technological development, it is not enough just to maintain present levels of employment and production." The Congress must be prepared and willing "to move quickly to adopt programs in the interest of economic expansion."

The Committee Report reveals a growing awareness that the conventional budget is obsolete for purposes of policy decisions. The Committee, in discussing tax policy, concentrated its attention on the cash budget.

The Committee was in favor of increasing public works to meet the needs of a growing population and an expanding economy. It recognized that the nation has fallen behind in schools, highways, hospitals, and other community facilities. Slum clearance and public housing must move forward more rapidly. The Federal government should make important contributions. The financing should be direct from the Treasury and not from indirect authorities.

The Committee recommended acceleration of public works and felt it imperative that an Office of Coordination of Public Works Planning be set up as proposed by the Committee last year and now proposed by the President. The Committee urged loans, technical assistance, and area-development programs for distressed areas.

The Committee boldly pushed ahead of the Executive and set up extensive and carefully planned hearings on (a) foreign economic policy, (b) tax policy, (c) economic stabilization, (d) economic statistics, and (e) low-income families.

A supplementary report by the Democrats noted that the built-in stabilizers, now happily accepted by all, were adopted "over bitter Republican opposition." In a more nonpartisan spirit they found this year's Report of the President a concrete expression of progress in economic understanding. "It recognizes, more than the preceding Report, the active role of government in cushioning the effect of declines on private economic activity." It frankly and forthrightly accepts compensatory fiscal policy. "It is especially reassuring to find running throughout the entire Report evidences of an increasing acceptance of the theory that the balanced budget, 'hard money,' and the reconstruction of the Federal debt structure are not to be regarded as ends in themselves." Unfortunately, said the Democrats, the practices of the Administration have not always been consistent with these recently embraced theories.

Despite the "high professional competence which marks the analysis in the current Economic Report, the Committee unanimously felt it appropriate, in the interest of continued improvement of the Employment Act machinery, to comment upon several of the Report's deficiencies."

Especially important, it was felt, was the fact that the

President's Report did not clearly state that the economy can safely meet even greater military burdens if these are needed for security. On a different plane it was stressed that the Committee cannot intelligently evaluate the President's Report if it does not contain (*a*) numerical estimates of levels of employment and production needed to carry out the Act's objectives and (*b*) estimates of foreseeable trends. "The philosophy of the Act clearly is that measurements be made. The economic garment, it is recognized, should be 'tried on for size' before alterations are made. Otherwise a year may pass before one is able to recognize an ill-fitted misshapen garment." The Council's distaste for economic projections "has fallen before its own admission that such projections must be made in the discharge of its responsibilities."

Several Republican members—Watkins, Flanders, Goldwater, and Wolcott—defended, in a supplementary statement, at some length the omission in the Economic Report of numerical projections. This defense consisted primarily of quotations from the testimony of the Council chairman, who explained that these projections, while used by the Council itself, should not be included in the President's Report because they were necessarily based on a range of assumptions about the growth of the labor force and increases in man-hour productivity.

E. *Words versus Deeds*

Finally we come to the President's 1956 Report. The President claimed that his Administration had sought to discharge its responsibilities through a series of closely related policies. The Administration had kept the economy strong and growing by restricting governmental expenditures yet adding (*sic*) to the stock of public assets, especially highways, hospitals, and educational facilities. (An informed reader will certainly rub his eyes at this point.) Almost equally arresting is the claim that the ties of trade and investment with other nations had been extended. (Beyond the marks, one may ask, set by Hull and Marshall?) Also it was alleged that the impact of blighted neighborhoods, illness, and unemployment had been tempered.

Knowing how little had in fact been done, what should one say about these assertions? Equally difficult would be the task of spelling out what content could be put into the claim that the "automatic workings" of our fiscal system *have been extended*.

The points made by the President with respect to the Administration's responsibility "to pursue policies that will help to keep the private economy strong and growing" straddle between (*a*) the old die-hard viewpoint that the best way to strengthen the economy is to give it utmost freedom to go it on its own and (*b*) the view that a strong economy under modern conditions requires a partnership between government and private enterprise, with the government playing a vigorous role in the mixed public-private economy of today. Pride was taken in the removal of the price and wage controls instituted during the Korean War (controls which were never intended to be permanent) and restricting public expenditures (primarily a result of the cessation of active hostilities). But what about the civilian areas in which increased expenditures are sorely needed? The past hard-fought progress made toward the mixed public-private economy of the modern welfare state was somewhat parsimoniously accepted. There was but meager recognition that there is still much unfinished business. Social priorities and the optimum use of productive resources received scant notice.

The President's Report was quite satisfied with the nature of the great 1955 recovery despite the fact that it was sparked primarily by a 40 per cent increase in automobile-installment credit and a 30 per cent increase in real-estate credit.[2] There are surely sounder ways of promoting recovery than abnormal and nonmaintainable credit spurts.

With respect to tax adjustments, no clear-cut statement is made of the compensatory-tax principle. Instead, it is made to appear (p. 31) that the balanced-budget principle and the compensatory-tax principle reinforce each other. This is particularly unfortunate in view of the fact that both in the State of the Union message and in the Budget message the balanced-budget principle, and not the compensatory-tax principle, was set forth as the appropriate criterion for tax policy. Instead of arguing that tax cuts should be made if the economy turns down, precisely the opposite position was taken in these two Reports, namely, that if booming tax revenues create a surplus, taxes may justifiably be cut.

Broadening the scope of prosperity is envisaged in terms of agricultural policy, help for distressed areas in the form of technical assistance and lending for capital improvements, making more effective use of Federal programs already in existence, improving the economic status of older persons, and finally by highly cautious suggestions about ways and means of "coping with personal hardships," including such matters as floods and temporary disability.

In the chapter on Building for Future Prosperity the principle is firmly set down that the budget should be balanced "surely over a term of very few years." There is no recognition that this may not at all be appropriate policy in an economy capable of doubling the GNP in twenty or twenty-five years—an economy which may well need even more than a proportionate increase in money and liquid assets. It is assumed that the policy of lengthening the maturities of the government's outstanding debt is obviously a good long-run policy.

[2] It was recognized (p. 32) that the increase in installment consumer debt was the largest on record in so brief a period.

It is assumed that the Federal government can meet its obligations in a rapidly growing economy with a "modest enlargement of essential Federal expenditures within the framework of a balanced budget" (p. 75). It is assumed that it would be unmistakably good policy to begin reducing our huge public debt (p. 76). Support is given to the confused notion that such reductions would surely contribute to our children's economic future (p. 76).

There is a section on Home Ownership and Improving Neighborhoods, and appropriate recognition is given to the immense role played by the Federal Housing Administration and Veterans' Administration programs, and some good things are said about the urban renewal program. It was noted that home ownership has increased from 41 per cent in 1940 to 57 per cent in 1955—a tribute to the importance of governmental policy. There was finally a discussion (highly disappointing in real content) about enlarging public assets—public works, schools, hospitals, highways, water resources, etc.

There was talk of boldness, but the will to act seemed lacking. There was no disposition to embark on new adventures in social and economic policy commensurate with the needs of a growing and changing economy. In social politics one has to run fast to stay in the same place.

F. The Joint Committee Has Its Say

The Report of the Joint Committee, March, 1956, is of interest on several counts. It noted that the tenth anniversary of the Employment Act finds the objectives and machinery of the Act firmly established. The Report, without a single dissenting vote, stated firmly that the basic guide to Federal fiscal policy should be the state of the National Economy. This is highly significant, since the State of the Union and Budget messages had plumped for the *balanced budget* as the appropriate guide to fiscal policy.

The Committee noted the widely held view that there was a good deal of internal inconsistency in the economic assumptions underlying the President's Budget message and his Economic Report; and it expressed the view that the Council of Economic Advisers should take the leadership in efforts to coordinate the assumptions underlying the various Presidential reports. Referring to the excessive liberalization of consumer installment credit, the Committee stated that unless private enterprise exercises self-discipline, it may be necessary to reestablish stand-by Federal authority.

The Democratic members of the Committee made a unanimous supplementary report. They noted with gratification that the President's 1955 Report "represented progress in economic understanding by the Administration." But they felt unable to express the same satisfaction with respect to the 1956 Report. Instead of a scholarly contribution to economic understanding, they found it burdened throughout with strong political overtones.

Immediately they seized upon the series of ten "closely related policies" through which the Administration claimed to have discharged its responsibilities. A mere listing of desirable programs offers, they said, no evidence of how vigorously they are to be pursued. The basic test, said the Democratic members, is whether budget provisions have been made to carry the programs into effect. They then proceeded to examine the budget and found that it provided a mere $300 million (less than one-tenth of one per cent of GNP) for the so-called "new and expanded programs for enhancing opportunities for human well-being and economic growth." And even this modest sum could not be counted on unless the Congress increased the postal rates by $350 million. Looking up the counterpart of these recommended programs in the Budget message, they found that for some there was no provision whatever for Federal funds, others were not to go into effect until later fiscal years, and in other cases the amounts to be spent were very minute indeed. The test of the effectiveness of these programs, they asserted, is not the elegance of the language with which they are described but the actual effort put into their achievement.[3]

The Democratic members found it difficult to understand the President's plea for restricting expenditures while at the same time admitting that we must increase expenditures for schools, highways, and medical facilities if economic growth is not to be seriously retarded. The President had urged "staying within the limits of Federal revenues." The Democratic members believed that we should rather set the expenditures at the levels necessary to "make up for the neglects of the past" and then make adequate financial provision to carry them out. They saw a backlog of school-construction needs, a critical shortage of scientifically trained personnel, a clogging of the nation's highway system, a need to raise the nation's health standards. They believed that our cultural advances should keep pace with our natural progress. They found little in the actual program of the President with respect to needed advances to temper the impact of unemployment, old age, illness, and blighted neighborhoods. They found the public-housing program inadequate. They called the depressed-area loan fund of $50 million to be matched 3 to 1 from other sources "disastrously inadequate."

Finally, the Democratic members reiterated in a firm state-

[3] Senator Paul Douglas has put this in somewhat more spicy language as follows: "One of the things I don't like about this Administration is the deviousness of its operators; the pretentiousness that they are doing something when they are doing nothing or moving in the opposite direction; the air of unctuousness with which they will sabotage good causes while giving verbal adherence to them" (*New York Times*, May 16, 1956).

ment their belief that "fiscal integrity, if it is not to be a hollow phrase, calls for using the Federal government's fiscal powers deliberately in such a way as to minimize economic fluctuations from the path of steady growth." "The Secretary of the Treasury," they noted, "apparently does not now accept this generally held principle of fiscal policy."

G. *Ten Years under the Employment Act*

One is tempted to draft a summary of critical conclusions. This, however, is not necessary. The survey speaks for itself, and the result is far from being altogether reassuring. One is enormously impressed with the infinite complexity of economic life. The task of guiding a dynamic and rapidly changing economy is immeasurably difficult. Let him who is without sin cast the first stone.

One thing is certain. We have yet to face the real test. That will come when we face a substantial decline in aggregate investment in fixed capital—plant, equipment, construction of all kinds, housing.

The really big events were partly guided by wise planning and partly by accident. As I see it, they include the following: (1) the reconversion policies of 1945–1946, (2) the tax cut of 1948, (3) the $10 billion shift in the fiscal position of the Federal government in 1949, (4) the veterans' dividend in early 1950, (5) the pay-as-you-go taxes of 1950–1951, (6) the dramatic change-over to monetary ease by the Federal Reserve in the spring of 1953, (7) the tax reductions of 1953–1954.

Good points have been scored, and mistakes have been made. Yet mistakes per se are not serious. The unforgivable sin is to stick stubbornly to a line of policy which the flow of events proves to be wrong. Turning a sensitive cheek to changes in wind direction—a quick readiness to make a policy shift—this is perhaps the chief virtue.

CHAPTER 8

STANDARDS AND VALUES
IN A RICH SOCIETY

A. The Eradication of Poverty and the Role of Capital Formation

In this chapter I turn to matters related to but still somewhat beyond the range of the economist. It is not enough to rescue economics, as Keynes sought to do, from the narrow role assigned to it by Marshall—essentially a branch of business cost accounting—and restore it to the loftier plane of Political Economy or, as Adam Smith so aptly put it—The Wealth of Nations. Economics must concern itself with something more than merely maximum output and full employment. It must also concern itself with social priorities. In other words, it must, in a sense, become a branch of moral philosophy, as Adam Smith indeed had it.

In the last half-century the American Economy has lifted the standard of living of the mass population to undreamed-of levels of comfort and luxury. Mass poverty has largely been wiped out.

Full employment has been a major factor, perhaps *the* major factor, in overcoming widespread economic distress during the last fifteen years. Serious distress is indeed a function of *low* incomes, but it is also a function of *unstable* income. The periodic complete loss of income, often lasting over prolonged periods of depression, has throughout our history been a leading cause of destitution.

Still, full employment in a poor country will not cure poverty. The eradication of poverty depends basically upon science, technical progress, and capital accumulation. Without a large stock of capital goods poverty could not be eliminated. Yet this accumulated stock creates not a few of our problems.

The recent literature on growth and rising living standards has had a great deal to say about the ratio of the aggregate capital stock to real income. The comparative stability of this capital-output ratio over the long run has well-nigh led some economists to forget the law of diminishing marginal productivity. It is just not true that one can continue to build more and more plants and more and more equipment and out of this process grow richer and richer. Historically, the capital-output ratio has indeed been fairly stable,[1] but this is only because, whenever the declining marginal productivity of capital sets in, investment falls off, and so a new balance is reached.

Observing the historical ratio of capital to output, it is very easy to fall into the error which currently we frequently encounter, namely, that *any* desired rate of growth in our standard of living is possible if we but push the rate of investment hard enough. If the historical rate of capital accumulation has made possible an increase in output of, say, 3½ per cent per annum, why then, it is asked, should we not double the rate and thereby obtain an annual rate of growth in living standards of, say, 7 per cent per annum? If output is a function of the rate of capital accumulation, there would be virtually no limit to the rate of long-term growth. We might, it would seem, enjoy any desired rate of growth if we were only pre-

[1] Actually the ratio has apparently declined some from around 3 to 3.5 per cent in 1880–1915 to perhaps 2.8 to 3.0 in 1949–1955.

pared to push investment to the limit. Some recent pronouncements from high government officials stem, I suggest, from this philosophy.

For the moment let us concentrate attention on long-term growth. I am here considering this problem in terms of per capita growth. What now are the real bases of long-term growth? The answer, I believe, is not capital accumulation, though this plays a necessary, albeit restricted, role. The answer, I suggest, is rather scientific research and invention. If these can be made to grow at a more rapid rate than in the past, then we shall in the usual case be able to open up deeper and broader outlets for investment and thereby accelerate the rate of long-term growth.[1a] These new outlets would probably, but not necessarily, raise the ratio of investment to GNP to a figure higher than the long-term maintainable rate which has been found to be feasible in the past.

Recently, however, we have been talking altogether too much, I feel, not about ways and means of opening investment outlets, but merely about ways and means of artificially stimulating investment. Accelerated depreciation is a case in point. This could, of course, be applied in a cyclically stabilizing manner. But this has not been done. Instead, the measure recently adopted is in effect a subsidy which, made continuously, without regard to cyclical fluctuations, would tend to push investment faster than otherwise beyond the maintainable rate.

It would, of course, be quite possible to carry the process of subsidization of investment very much farther than is contemplated with respect to the accelerated-depreciation device.

[1a] Public investment can often unlock large private investment opportunities. Power development can never be carried to the full on the narrow principle of a self-liquidating project. Full development requires that cognizance be taken of the *indirect* effect of such programs upon the productivity of the *community as a whole*. Only the government can take this larger view. Even the Public Power people have never fully grasped this principle.

Indeed it could be carried to almost any desired point. The rate of obsolescence and replacement would thereby be greatly accelerated. We could, if we wished to, increase the rate of capital replacement to a point at which no house would be more than, say, fifteen years old, no plant more than, say, ten years old, and no machinery more than, say, two years old, or even farther. If we are prepared to restrict our consumption with sufficient severity, we could acquire, at least in the United States, an incredible degree of "newness" or "youth" in our stock of fixed capital goods.

Such a program would, however, clearly involve a highly wasteful use of resources. We would be spending a very high proportion of our productive power merely to scrap useful and comparatively new plant and equipment. We would indeed enjoy the possession of a strictly up-to-date stock of fixed capital all around. But the price we would pay for this artificial "newness" would necessarily be a lower output of consumers' goods. Americans love gadgets. Farmers are sometimes so enamored with the sight of expensive and uneconomical machinery that they are prepared to sacrifice their standard of living and that of their families to get it. And many urban families are prepared to sacrifice almost anything to get an expensive new car.

In the United States we have reached a level of productivity so high that we could, if we wanted to, devote perhaps *half* of our resources to a highly accelerated rate of obsolescence and to an extravagantly large accumulation of very new capital goods. But the price would be a severely restricted output of services and of nondurable and semidurable consumers' goods.

Clearly we should not aim at the *maximum* rate of capital accumulation. We should aim at the *optimum* rate. And that optimum rate would be determined, I suggest, first, by the rate of scientific research and invention and, second, by the growth of population.

Scientific research and invention are indeed likely, as I have already indicated, to open up larger investment outlets, but not necessarily so. Scientific research and invention may at times increase productivity yet lessen the need for capital accumulation. Moreover, expenditures in human resources—education, health, etc.—may not only directly contribute to living standards but may also, no less than capital accumulation, increase the productive capacity of the society. There is far too great a tendency nowadays to plead for policies that encourage investment in material capital goods—plant and equipment—and to forget that outlays on the improvement of our human resources may be even more productive. We are concerned altogether too much about increased investment in brick and mortar and not enough about investments designed to improve the quality and productivity of our people.

B. The Rise in Living Standards

Income per family in real terms is now about two and a half times as high as at the beginning of this century. This represents a gain in real purchasing power of 1¾ per cent per annum. At the same time working hours have been reduced from around 60 per week to 40 per week; from a ten-hour day and a six-day week to an eight-hour day and a five-day week. The gain in leisure time is clearly one of the best indices of a higher standard of living.

Still the impressive rise in purchasing-power income requires at least some qualification. A calculation based on money income and price changes is not altogether convincing. In the nineteenth-century rural society many things were free which we now have to pay for. Consider the amount of labor which must be devoted in modern communities, not to positive productive effort, but to neutralizing the disagreeable consequences of dense concentrations of population in large urban communities. Much effort is devoted, not to providing utilities, but to the removal of disutilities, by-products of industrialization and urbanization. Yet the labor expended on the removal of disutilities is counted in our money economy as a part of our Gross National Product.

Industrialized cities with overcrowded tenement districts have made an effort via public parks to recover *some* of the lost sunshine, open fields, and fresh air formerly enjoyed by rural populations. Yet in many communities the parks are not located where people live, where children can have direct access to them. Instead of big and grand parks we need many small neighborhood parks, not for an outing but for daily use, not for an occasional automobile drive but for continuous recreation.

Thus it is that our ugly industrial cities scarcely help to build up a convincing case that our standard of living is as far above that of fifty or a hundred years ago as the figures of money incomes corrected for price changes would indicate. In 1900, 60 per cent of our population lived in rural areas and only 22 per cent in cities of over 25,000. Now only 40 per cent live in rural areas, and 60 million people live in cities of over 25,000. The terrific problems of providing urban transportation involve a vast investment of capital and labor. And while the work week is far shorter, should we not add back some part of the hours spent in the nerve-racking rush to get to and from work? In these terms there are still many people who have what in fact amounts to a ten-hour day.

In realistic terms, changes in the standard of living can perhaps best be measured in terms of food consumption, housing, health, education, recreation, and leisure.

Changes in the consumption of food disclose clearly a rising living standard. While the consumption of meat per capita was slightly lower in 1950 than in 1900, the consumption of vegetables is nearly 50 per cent higher, fresh fruits 15 per cent higher, cheese 60 per cent higher, and chicken and turkeys 70 per cent higher. These increases, combined with a drastic decline in the consumption of wheat flour—the main item, along with potatoes, in a poor man's diet—disclose a richer and more nutritive diet. In addition to the varied items of diet already referred to, the consumption of such nutrients as vitamin A, thiamine, ascorbic acid, calcium, and riboflavin have increased around 30 per cent per capita. A man is no longer old at fifty, as was the case seventy-five years ago. We have achieved a far healthier diet during the last fifty or seventy-five years. Considerations such as these are useful supplements to mere monetary aggregates.[2]

The American people are certainly better housed now than fifty years ago. Plumbing, electric lights, and central heating are indicative of this advance. Yet even today we have over 7 million substandard dwelling units which ought at once to be demolished, either because they are without toilet, bath, running water, or are otherwise dilapidated. Kerosene stoves still heat a high proportion of the homes in many working-class sections—a major cause of fires. To complete the task of raising housing standards to the minimum of decency for all would require, it is estimated by the Twentieth Century Fund,[3] around $85 billion. There is still a good deal of unfinished business before we can say that the American people are well housed. Nonetheless, there is a vast difference between the housing facilities available to the American wage-earning family today compared with the situation around 1890, when Jacob Riis gave his lurid description of *How the Other Half Lives*.

So familiar have we become with the widespread use of electrical household appliances that we are prone to think that

[2] *America's Needs and Resources,* Twentieth Century Fund, 1955, chap. 5.
[3] *Ibid.,* p. 512.

all Americans are now equipped with these comforts. Yet 50 per cent do not have vacuum cleaners, 30 per cent do not have electric washing machines, and 20 per cent are without electric refrigerators.[4] Still, apart from food and housing and more leisure time, the most conspicuous gains, no doubt, for the great majority are the mechanical gadgets, comforts, and luxuries—household appliances, plumbing, the automobile, the motion picture, radio, and television.

C. Mass Education

The substitution of mechanical power for human power and the consequent gains in productivity have not only reduced the work week from 60 to 40 hours; they have also made possible a much longer period of education for the whole population. In this respect we have witnessed a truly revolutionary development since 1900, indeed since 1910. As late as 1910 only 5 per cent of the youth of college age (18 to 21) attended college. By 1950 it was 30 per cent.[5] As late as 1910 only a few went on to high school. Then the flood began. Already by 1920 high-school graduations per capita had doubled, and by 1940 the number graduating from high school each year was, per capita, eight times that of 1900. And by 1950 the number of graduations from colleges and universities, on a per capita basis, had reached eight times that of 1900.

This massive increase in high-school and college attendance has come upon us all of a sudden in the last few decades. Indeed throughout the nineteenth century a high proportion of American children had only four or five years of schooling and often no more than four or five months per year. Today high-school attendance is 6,600,000. Fifty years ago it was

[4] *Ibid.*, p. 242.

[5] James B. Conant, *Education and Liberty*, Harvard University, 1953, p. 35.

only 700,000. Today college and university attendance is 3,000,000; in 1900 it was only 240,000.

Nothing else like it has occurred in any other part of the world. We have not had time to make the proper adjustments. This flood of students into secondary schools and higher institutions has come upon us in a single generation. It is no wonder that our high-school standards are low. No nation could train an adequate number of competent teachers in so short a time. Worse yet, we have miserably failed to give teachers the salary differential needed to draw the best brains into the teaching profession. On the stage we ridicule schoolma'ams, and in the market place we underprice them.

The task of education is, moreover, enormously complicated by the heterogeneity of our population and the difficult problem of immigrant adjustment to American life. Forty-five million immigrants have stormed our shores during the last hundred years. In 1900, 40 per cent of the whole population was foreign-born, or born of foreign parents, and the figure is still 25 per cent today.

D. *The Submerged Tenth in a Rich Society*

This mass immigration explains in no small measure the extraordinary spread between the median income in the United States and the income of the lowest decile. And it accounts in considerable degree for many personal and family maladjustments and social dislocations.

What was it that caused this massive movement of people from the Old World to the New? It was primarily the revolutionary increase in population which occurred in Europe throughout the nineteenth century. From 1800 to 1910 the population of the five largest European countries—England, France, Italy, Germany, and Russia—increased from 125 million to 325 million. The chief cause was the sharp decline in the death rate. The struggle for existence grew desperate. Subdivision of the family plots pushed down the subsistence level. Peasants by the millions were forced off the land. In America they crowded, after the 1880s, into our great urban industrial centers. Uprooted from their Old World peasant communities, where human ties were close and moral values were firmly fixed, they were all at sea in a new and strange world. The uprooted immigrant had to readjust his peasant outlook on life.[6] He had to come to terms with an urbanized industrialism.

To make matters still worse, a psychological conflict, placing severe strains on parental discipline, inevitably developed between the immigrant and his children—a conflict born of differences in language and social environment. The restraints and security of the Old World peasant communities were missing. Sheds, shanties, stables, and cellars were drafted for living space in our great industrial centers. The crowded street was the only playground.[7] Out of such conditions have grown psychopathic disorders and social maladjustments. It is true that those endowed with exceptional energy and capacity, both mental and physical, found in the American environment almost boundless opportunities and rose very rapidly to higher social and economic levels. More gradually the great middle group also improved its status and succeeded reasonably well in the difficult process of amalgamation and assimilation. But there was also the submerged tenth or quintile.

The physical and mental deficiencies which we find today among the lower two deciles of our population stem in part at least from the conflicts experienced by the uprooted peasant immigrant unable to find his way about in congested cities

[6] Oscar Handlin, *The Uprooted*, Little, Brown & Company, 1952.

[7] I note even today, as I walk around the streets of some of our great cities, that school children in recess time have frequently no place to play except on pavement and adjoining sidewalks.

amid the uncertainties and insecurity of a laissez-faire industrialism. Against the background of these conditions one can
learn a good deal that explains the submerged decile in a rich
society.

Our much-heralded high *average* income is indeed the envy
of even high-standard countries, but astonishment is often
the reaction one gets to the incredibly wide spread between the
median income in the United States and the income of the
lowest decile. Not only have we been historically the country
with the widest cyclical swings; we have also exhibited the
widest spread between income classes, especially at the bottom of the scale.

In the United States today there are 8,000,000 families and
individual household units with a money income of less than
$1,000 per year and an additional 6,500,000 with incomes
between $1,000 and $2,000. A considerable proportion live in
depressed areas, where unemployment is chronic even when
the nation as a whole is enjoying full-employment opportunities. It is a vicious circle. Because the area is depressed,
public revenues are limited. Community services, and especially the quality of education, are seriously deficient. Such
areas become not merely economically depressed areas; they
become also derelict areas, composed of a population with
inferior education and lacking in physical and mental vigor.
The able, aggressive young people migrate. Those who remain
behind constitute, disproportionately, aged persons, remaining
members of broken families, and generally persons inade-
quately equipped to compete successfully in modern industry.

In part it is a rural problem, and in part it is a race problem.
Two-thirds of the low-income rural families live in the South.
Moreover, the incidence of low incomes among rural families
is twice as great among Negroes as among whites.

Lack of education is a primary cause of low income. Low-
income families are compelled to spend a disproportionate per

cent of their income on food and housing. There is little left for education. Substandard families spend 65 per cent of their income on food and housing, while wage-earning families in general spend only 45 per cent on these two consumption categories. Moreover, as I have already indicated, such families are likely to live in communities where educational facilities are very limited.

The problem of education for the children of low-income families is far more important to the nation as a whole than appears on the surface. An alarmingly high proportion of the nation's children are reared in low-income families. In general there is an inverse correlation between income and size of family. Thus families with five children have a median income of $3,155, while families with two children have a median income of $4,500. The bulk of the nation's children grow up in relatively low-income families with three, four, five, six, or more children. Indeed, of the 55 million children under eighteen years of age, 30 million are reared in families with three or more children. Of these about 16 million, or about 30 per cent of all the nation's children, live in the eighteen lowest-income states. Several of these states have a per capita income less than half that of the richest states.

These poorer states cannot, without substantial Federal aid, provide the minimum American standards of education, health, and social welfare. These children are Americans. Yet citizens of New York and Massachusetts are prone to talk and act as though they were foreigners. We are indeed almost immeasurably distant from being *world* citizens. In the present stage of human development this is at least understandable. But is it not incredible that we pretend to be citizens of our separate states and not citizens of the United States when we consider the problem of adequate minimum standards of education for Americans everywhere?

The wide spread between the median income and the lowest

decile in our society holds not only with respect to income and education but also with respect to physical fitness. Not only is the rate of illiteracy high in the lower deciles, but the extraordinary high proportion of our total youth physically and mentally unfit for military service is clearly in some part to be explained by the unfavorable economic and social conditions under which the lower deciles of our population live. Our slums persist in the midst of a $400 billion GNP. It is true that the problem of juvenile delinquency is a very complicated one and can by no means be explained simply in terms of income status. Nonetheless, it cannot be denied that our slums contribute not a little to the problem. Slum clearance and a nationwide system of health insurance are high in the agenda of unfinished business.

It is not only the personal incomes and the physical and mental status of the submerged tenth which are seriously deficient. It is also their opportunity to share in the amenities of life which only the community can offer. Our great cities lack adequate parks and playgrounds—Cambridge, Mass., is a notorious example—and they lack community facilities for recreation and social life. The joy of living in a city with beautiful parks within the reach of all and with easy and quick access to the surrounding countryside is something that our lower-income groups do not share in equal measure with comparable income groups in Holland, Switzerland, Denmark, and Sweden.

Joyful living is not simply an individual matter. Among the more important amenities of life are those which only the community can provide. This is a job for government. And if we hide behind the doctrine that all this is no affair of the Federal government, we become in practice pure defeatists. I am glad to note, in this connection, the splendid work of the Joint Congressional Committee on the Economic Report with respect to the problems of the low-income families and ways and means of dealing with these problems at the Federal level.

The lower-income classes are at a peculiar disadvantage because of the preoccupation of the American society with mechanical gadgets and because of the relatively slight emphasis placed upon social values and community activities. We are increasingly in danger of making our economic system a mere treadmill. We have reached a point in our development where mere emphasis on larger and larger output of mechanical gadgets becomes rather meaningless, if, indeed, not a detriment to truly satisfactory living. We spend billions and billions of dollars on automobiles, of which perhaps half is frittered away on mere size, gadgets, and chrome—all of which add little to the social utility of comfortable transportation. And expenditures on automobiles, not including operation or the vast sums spent on roads, are twice as great as the aggregate expenditure on schools, including school construction and other capital outlays for education.

The average public-school teacher's salary is $3,450, while the average full-time wage for production workers in manufacturing industry is $3,735, and that for railroad production workers (not including supervising employees) is $4,100. A country as rich as ours can and should make the school teacher's profession highly attractive financially. A good rule, and a thoroughly justifiable one, would be an average salary scale twice that of production workers. This means more than a doubling of school teachers' salaries. In ten years we should see a profound change in the quality of our teachers. To say that we can't afford it is nonsense. Eight years hence, by 1965, we can produce a GNP of $550 billion. That is $150 billion more than now. We are spending currently a paltry $3½ billion on public-school teachers' salaries. We can well afford to double or treble that amount out of our rapidly increasing national income.

We shall not solve the problem of education for the submerged tenth or the lowest quintile until we have solved it for all the people. The same holds for youth programs, recreational facilities, and a nationwide system of health insurance.

E. What Goals Do We Seek?

After ten years of almost incredible *output* performance, we need to assess not merely the speed of our growth and progress but also the direction in which we are going. What *qualitative* goals shall we set up? What kind of country do we wish to build? These are matters that we dare not overlook, lest we perish, as a great nation, in the midst of material plenty.

Now someone will surely say: "What right has this armchair professor to talk about how the American public should use its resources? Leave it to the market to take care of all that." Superficially that sounds good, but in fact that answer will not do. The "market" cannot decide how much we shall spend on schools, on social security, or on national security. We have reached a point in our economic and social evolution where *social-value* judgments, not the market, must control the uses to which we put something like one-fourth of our productive resources. Our economy is no longer wholly a market economy. It is a mixed public-private economy.

And how are these social-value judgments to be determined? Do we leave it to chance, to nature, to the elemental, uneducated instincts of people? That indeed is the rule among savages. But civilized countries follow another rule, and it is this: "Train up a child in the way he should go, and when he is a man he will not depart therefrom." Civilized countries mold their people into civilized ways of thinking, guided by values that experience and knowledge have laid down. We don't leave it to the market. We educate. Only in this way can we achieve the great goals of a civilized society.

Here I come to a critical point. Our schools and churches can no longer be said to constitute the main educational media in this country. Modern technology has largely supplanted these older media. Children, young people, and grownups devote more hours per day the year round to the radio and television and the movies than they do to school, churches, or to reading. These mechanical media have become an important, if indeed not the most important, element in our entire educational process. And what worries me is this. These powerful educational media are controlled, not by educators, but by advertisers whose primary purpose is profit, not education. Advertisers do not control the editorials or news columns of our newspapers, though there may be an indirect influence. But they do control our radio and television programs. Is it any wonder that we prefer longer and longer cars with more and more chrome to good schools and well-paid teachers? At the very least, advertisers should not, I suggest, be allowed to sponsor or select the programs other than their own commercials.

We have been brought up with a narrow conception of the functions of public education. Adult education, music, drama, the fine arts, deserve public support. Even our F.M. fine music programs are painfully encroached upon by advertising.

Thus the problem of social priorities is hard upon us. It is not enough to achieve maximum employment and production. It is not enough to have quantitative goals. We cannot allow full employment to become merely a device to make our economy an efficient treadmill.

America's Needs and Resources discloses (p. 512) that the estimated cost of urban redevelopment in general—including a demolition of our 7 million slum houses—would amount to no more than the equivalent of about two years of defense expenditures at current levels.

In terms of GNP we are spending currently only 40 per

cent as much on hospitals today as in 1920–1924 (p. 312). We are spending (including operating and capital expenditures) only 2¼ per cent of our GNP on public schools, elementary and secondary. Indeed, in relation to GNP we are spending 20 per cent less on schools today than we spent twenty-five years ago. A rich country can't afford good schools and good teachers!

This is an area in which economists have been, I feel, neglectful of their duty. We need more study of social priorities.

Yet with all our distorted values there is happily a growing realization that we *have* accumulated a large backlog of long-range public-investment needs. This means larger and larger Federal budgets, not only absolutely but also in relation to the GNP. When I say "public investment" I mean not merely public works and resource-development projects. I include investment in human resources as well—schools, scholarship programs, medical research, a nationwide system of health insurance, recreational facilities, etc.

The problem of long-range public-investment planning is all the more important in view of our large and now again increasing defense and foreign-aid budgets. The national-security budgets compete with the growing urgent need for much larger long-range social-welfare budgets. I think we should all agree that national security comes first. Indeed I have never been able to understand why we continually debate the question whether our military strength is more or less equal to that of the Soviet Union when we, in fact, have ample resources to ensure our superiority by a wide margin. Our military program should be adequate to guarantee without question the peace of the world for the visible future. I am not, therefore, suggesting that we should reduce our military program. But I do, nonetheless, say that we should increase *now* by a substantial amount our long-range public-welfare budgets. That may involve a reappraisal of tax cuts. We are in a situation in which the marginal *tax* dollar can clearly yield a much higher social utility than the marginal *pay-envelope* dollar.

Let it be noted that the growing ratio of government purchases of goods and services—a trend which has been going on throughout our history—does indeed point up the unmistakable *fact* that our economy is becoming more and more a mixed public-private economy. But government ownership and operation of the means of production—the classical definition of socialism—is *not* noticeably on the increase. It is the welfare state that is growing, not the government as owner or operator. The welfare state is primarily a redistributor of income and a colossal purchaser of the products of private enterprise. But private enterprise does the job.

The growth of public budgets means that the public *finance* method of paying for goods and services will grow in relation to the *market-price* method. It does not mean that private enterprise is shrinking or that the tax base is shrinking. The goods are purchased from private enterprise. Thus private enterprise continues to grow in much the same proportion as the GNP. The welfare state does not in any appreciable degree operate to supplant the system of private enterprise. Instead it makes it stronger and more workable.

No one can dispute that we have become a rich society. We have made great advances on the purely economic plane. Unfortunately the progress we have made in many of the noneconomic aspects of life is limited, and in some areas we have, I fear, definitely retrogressed. The economic gains are visible on every hand. And economists, as a professional group, have, I think it is fair to say, contributed in no small measure to this development. Government departments have at long last been staffed with well-trained economists. State papers nowadays are mainly concerned with economic mat-

ters, often highly technical. Congressional hearings and legis-
lative programs draw increasingly on the work of economists
inside and outside the government. The result is evident in the
massive and highly technical messages and reports of the President to Congress.

Would that our colleagues, concerned with noneconomic
aspects of American life, could claim equal progress. We
are learning, in the midst of material plenty, that man "cannot
live by bread alone." How do educators feel when they contemplate the deterioration of our public schools; the social
psychologists and pathologists who observe the increase in
mental disorders, crime, and juvenile delinquency, or, on
another plane, the current predominance of neurotic art?

We have learned how to make a living; we have still to learn
how to live. Until we have eliminated the ugliness of our
great industrial cities we cannot claim to have reached as a
nation a truly high standard of living. America is long on
wealth but short on appreciation of the beautiful. Some years
ago I visited, in company with Professor Jørgen Pedersen, a
large farm in Jutland, Denmark. It employed eighteen or
twenty well-housed farm workers. Two of these devoted full
time to beautifying the place, to the flower gardens, the lawns,
the trees, the buildings. That farm was a place on which to
live, not merely a place to make a living.

Many readers have no doubt visited the famous Town Hall
in Stockholm, a noble work of man. Compare this with the
city hall in Boston, Mass., to take only one example.
The Town Hall in Stockholm is not simply a place where the
mayor has his office. It is a community building where citizens
of high or low rank can meet in civic-group gatherings amidst
an atmosphere of dignity, beauty, and elegance. Such things
make for the good life. A higher standard of mere material
wealth is no substitute for beauty—for the things of the mind
and the spirit.

Few will deny the cultural deficiencies of our cities and towns, and everyone will agree that an adequate program would cost a lot of money. And the answer to that usually is that we can't afford it. We are too poor! Ah, that is it. We have become so gadget-rich that we can't afford to build culturally rich communities. But what does it profit a man if he gain the whole world but lose his own soul?

CHAPTER 9

KEYNESIAN THINKING AND THE PROBLEMS OF OUR TIME

A. Introductory

An amazing thing about human beings is the rapidity with which they adjust to change once the ice of old conventions is broken. Things that formerly seemed incredible have come to pass—changes in our ways of thinking and, to some extent, in our institutions. Yet here they are, and nobody thinks a thing about it.

The public's reaction to new ideas typically passes through three stages: (1) Crazy. How silly can one become? (2) These ideas are dangerous. They must be vigorously opposed. (3) Why, of course! Who ever thought otherwise?

A conservative is a person who warmly and heartily approves of a reform measure ten years after it has been put into effect. I can't find the quotation, but a distinguished economist once said something like this: "A laissez-faire economy can best be defined as a society operating under man-made institutions and conventions to which people have long been accustomed."

I have just defined a conservative as a person who is ten years behind the times. That, of course, is paying him the compliment of being a highly intelligent conservative. Ten years is not a very long time in which to adapt oneself to drastic changes. For the run-of-the-mine conservative the time lag, as

American experience would indicate, is much longer—perhaps about twenty years or so. And for the professional economist, with his laboriously worked-out and firmly imbedded logic, not infrequently the time lag is even longer. Acceptance of change may indeed have to await a new generation.

The history of economics as a science discloses that its practitioners have not infrequently adjusted slowly to social change. Economic science could perhaps somewhat facetiously be defined as a rationalization of institutions and conventions thirty years after the event. Social innovation has not infrequently come from practical men of affairs. Indeed, many an important institutional change, at its inception, was roundly condemned by economists as dangerous and unworkable.

One of the most startling innovations of all time was the daring scheme of William Paterson back in 1694 to establish the Bank of England. Imagine what a professionally trained academic economist [1] would have said about a scheme to create money out of thin air! If I am not mistaken, when the first baseball curve was thrown in 1867 physicists explained that it was contrary to the laws of motion and just wasn't possible! Later, of course, rationalization caught up with experience. So also time and again in economics. Trade-unionism was springing up here and there not only in England but also in the United States in the first half of the nineteenth century and by 1870 was firmly and permanently established in England. For the professional economist, however, trade-unionism remained, as far as economic theory was concerned, pretty much of a conundrum, and it was not until Sidney and Beatrice Webb wrote their *Industrial Democracy* in 1897 that any serious economic analysis disclosing its role in a social democracy was made of this long-established institution.

[1] Note should be taken of the notable and ingenious work of Sir William Petty and Gregory King, contemporaries of William Paterson, who were developing the new science of "Political Arithmetik."

When Bismarck introduced social security in Germany in 1884–1887, the proposal certainly was no product of economic research. But some twenty years later Sir William Beveridge gave the social-security principle a generally acknowledged rationalization. And so it goes.

B. *Monetary Policy and the Treatise*

In this chapter I wish to consider the role that Keynes played in a changing world. I must, however, hasten to say that a great many of the social innovations of the last generation have little to do with Keynes. Keynes was not a reformer of the social-welfare type. All his life he was concerned with money and the flow of spending. All the way down to the publication of the *Treatise,* he concentrated on monetary reforms and central-bank management. The central bank, he thought, could control the rate of aggregate spending. After the *Treatise,* however, he was searching not merely for a *regulator* but for a *powerhouse* where the flow of aggregate spending could be generated. He found this in the fiscal operations of the government. Still, one of the indispensable pieces of machinery in this powerhouse was the central bank.

More than any other person in our generation, it was Keynes who drove home the point that a drastic remodeling of monetary and fiscal conventions was necessary if the system of private enterprise was to survive. Keynes' monetary and fiscal ideas were novel and often shocking. Today they have become commonplace.

There are today, as there have always been, different types of reformers. There are those who spin out dreams of a utopia consisting of ideal human beings of almost infinite good will. Economists, however, are typically rather hard-headed and can rarely be found in this camp. There is another type of reformer, much more common, who places his emphasis on the "rules of the game." Human beings, in the early days of economics as a science, could be moved about pretty much like chessmen. Thus the game could be played according to rules laid down by economists. So long as the rules were adhered to, the system would work. To the pure liberal economist (using the term in the French sense) the whole evolution of modern capitalism, especially during the last seventy-five years, is one big mistake. What is needed is a return to a truly competitive system. Things are going badly because the human animal refuses to act as economists think he ought to act. Organized groups render capitalism unworkable.

Now, that is one type of reformer. There is still another type—a reformer who is responsive to the historical process, who notes the stream of evolutionary forces at work and who contrives ways and means, not of suppressing these forces, but of guiding them toward a workable solution. "Individual capitalism," said Keynes, "has come to the point where it must apply itself to the scientific task of improving the structure of its economic machine." The proposals of this type of reformer survive because they are based on economic realism. They work with the tide of history, not against it. Keynes was this kind of reformer. Were this not so, despite all his brilliance, he would not today be the foremost architect of the economic reconstruction we have witnessed in this generation. In the words of Professor Pigou, "He was, beyond doubt or challenge, the most interesting, the most influential and the most important economist of his time." [2]

Now, someone will say that the very manner I have chosen to describe Keynes as an economic reformer proves that he really accomplished nothing. It was all in the cards. Everything that has happened was cast in the inexorable flow of

[2] *John Maynard Keynes*, A Memoir prepared by direction of the Council of King's College, Cambridge, 1949.

events. The gold standard was, in the nature of the case, doomed. It could not survive in the modern world. It was bound to go, Keynes or no Keynes. The balanced-budget dogma had to succumb to necessity. It has remained indeed a useful political screen, but in cold, practical politics it has become a maxim to be honored in the breach. The Keynesian analysis of full employment was surely, it is said, an intellectual rationalization of the irresistible drive of an awakened and determined democracy.

Thus it is argued on the one side that Keynes has ruined us, and on the other side that he has, in fact, accomplished nothing. Everything would have been as it is, Keynes or no Keynes. It is the old conundrum: Does history make the man, or does man make history?

The freedoms that we have we take for granted. Today we have a managed currency—complete freedom to create as much money and credit as we think wise. It was not always so. This is a truly revolutionary change in our economic system. But most of us have already forgotten that this freedom was acquired, so to speak, only yesterday. Anyone who may wish to revive his memory of the chains to which we were formerly tied, the grip of old conventions and the struggle required to free men's minds, can obtain a very good moving picture of the events by reading or re-reading Keynes' *Tract on Monetary Reform*, 1924; the various articles and pamphlets running from 1919 to 1932 (reprinted in his *Essays in Persuasion*) and the monetary sections in his *Treatise on Money* of 1930. These writings disclose Keynes in the midst of a great fight. It was no easy battle. It required the confidence of a fighter who believed himself equipped with weapons and skills superior to those which his opponents could muster. It took a certain arrogance. And of this Keynes had plenty!

Since the appearance of the *General Theory* we perhaps tend to underestimate the importance of Keynes' earlier work.

Very briefly his work as an economic reformer can be divided into two periods: (1) the twenties and early thirties and (2) after 1930. In the first period he knocked out the gold standard and all the postulates relating thereto. In the second period he knocked out the tenets of so-called sound finance. The fight against the gold standard was a general war, and the attack on the postulates relating thereto represented a number of separate battles. In the second period the attack centered on the dogma that governmental loan expenditures must necessarily curtail private spending, since, as was alleged, they drain off funds from the capital market. The first period represented a triumph for a managed currency; the second a triumph for (*a*) an active fiscal policy freed from the shackles that hitherto had bound us and (*b*) an economic justification for the redistributive processes of the welfare state designed to broaden and deepen the consumption base.

In the first period Keynes wrote, as already noted, the *Tract on Monetary Reform* and, scattered over the entire period, the numerous polemics against the return to the prewar gold parity, against deflation, against wage cutting, against giving priority to external stability in preference to internal stability, against emphasis on foreign investment rather than home investment, against submission to the dictates of the gold standard instead of equipping the economy with the powerful weapons of free monetary management.

In this first period Keynes was still, essentially, purely and simply a monetary theorist. The really important problems, he thought, were money, the bank rate, and the price level. After five years of dreadful unemployment he could still say, as late as 1925, that the central problem was stability of prices. We must find, he said, new policies and new instruments to control the working of economic forces. The opening stage of this political struggle, he said, centers about monetary policy. Indeed, the most violent interferences, he asserted, with stability and with justice were "precisely these which were brought about by changes in the price level." [3] Fluctuations in the price level encompassed, so he then thought, the whole of the economic problem. Far from standing apart from the reformist thinking which was fashionable in the twenties, he swam right in the middle of the stream along with Irving Fisher and Gustav Cassel, though he certainly kicked up more puddles than any of his contemporaries.

The economic machine was running downhill—deflation. This was the *cause*, he thought, of all the ills of the twenties and early thirties. There was nothing wrong with the economic structure, and indeed there was no need for any institutional reform whatsoever. The necessary machinery was already installed. The whole trouble was due to muddled thinking. The central bank, properly enlightened, could cure everything. The job of economic reform was simply to educate central bankers.

Note this rather remarkable fact. Keynes was never in the forefront of any *social* reform. I underline the word *social*. He was neither a Fabian socialist nor a supporter of labor-reform movements. In a lecture to the Liberal Summer School in 1925 he noted that the Labor party was a class party, and the class was not his class. "If I am going to pursue sectional interests at all," he said, "I shall pursue my own. I can be influenced by what seems to me to be Justice and good sense, but the Class War will find me on the side of the educated bourgeoisie." [4] Collective bargaining, trade-unionism,[5] minimum-wage laws, hours legislation, social security, a progressive tax system, slum

[3] *Essays in Persuasion*, p. 337.
[4] *Ibid.*, p. 324.
[5] In 1926, he wrote that trade unions, once the oppressed, have now become tyrants. The progressive liberal, he said, has the good advantage over the intelligent socialist that he does not have to give lip service to trade-union tyrannies, to the beauties of class war, or to doctrinaire state socialism.

clearance and housing, urban redevelopment and planning, educational reform—all these he accepted, but they were not among his preoccupations. In no sense could he be called the father of the welfare state.[6] He accepted welfare-state developments as part and parcel of the organic growth of capitalism. He was realistic. "The idea of the old-world party, that you can, for example, alter the value of money and then leave the consequential adjustments to be brought about by the forces of supply and demand, belongs," he said, "to the days of fifty or a hundred years ago when Trade Unions were powerless." [7] He accepted trade unions and labor legislation as a natural and perhaps inevitable development of the social order. If these new institutional developments created problems, it was the job of the economist, not to storm around thundering defiant predictions of doom if these obstacles to a free system were not cleaned out. It was the job of the economist to find ways and means of adjusting the economic machine so that it could operate effectively under the new conditions. But Keynes was not out fighting under the banners of labor reform or the welfare state. In politics he was a liberal. In economics he was at this stage a pure monetary theorist. We needed no new institutions. All we needed was freedom to act and the knowledge to manage our already established monetary and banking system.

Now, I do not wish to minimize Keynes' work in this first period. England was indeed following old monetary gods, and

[6] It is often said that the New Deal had little or nothing to do with Keynes' teaching. This is for the most part true. To illustrate, the social-security program in the United States was in no sense based on Keynes' *General Theory*. It was an American adaptation of European experience. It was a humanitarian reform often regarded as "good social ethics" but "bad economics." The *General Theory*, with its emphasis on the consumption function, taught us, however, that the social-security program was not only good social ethics but also good economics.

[7] *Essays in Persuasion*, p. 336.

the effect was disastrous. The return to the old gold parity was a frightful mistake. Nothing could illustrate more forcefully the penalty that must be paid for the social lag—the failure to keep pace with the flow of time.

Keynes, contrary to what is often said about him, had his feet firmly on the ground. He knew that to urge wage flexibility as the appropriate adjustment process, while seemingly good abstract theory, amounted in fact to no more than beating one's head against a stone wall. What England needed was not wage cutting but exchange-rate adjustment. Beyond that, having once achieved an equilibrium international position, she needed to free herself from the external domination imposed by the gold standard. She needed freedom to pursue the goal of internal stability. Having reached the trade-union and welfare stage in the evolution of modern capitalism, it was no longer feasible to permit the processes of adjustment to take the form of internal deflation. The position of international equilibrium, under modern conditions, could not be maintained by chaining the internal economy to external disturbances. Such a policy could only cause painful repercussions which might well destroy the system of private enterprise itself. Freedom of monetary management was, Keynes believed at this stage in his thinking, both the necessary and the sufficient condition for a workable capitalism. He was convinced that the economic policies followed by England all through the twenties and early thirties were all wrong. And he thought he had the remedy.

Now this leads us straight to the *Treatise on Money* of 1930. This work really included within its two bulky volumes three separate books. One, the briefest, was a pamphlet on Index Numbers. Other sections could well have been combined into a book on Monetary Management,[8] including an analysis of the role of banks as creators of money, reserve

[8] Actually Books I, V, and VII in the *Treatise*.

money and bank money, savings deposits and cash deposits, and the problems of central-bank management. These constituted, so to speak, a textbook on money and banking.

But what really intrigued Keynes was obviously the theoretical part dealing with his fundamental equations and the savings and investment problem. These sections in fact constituted a separate book on the business cycle, or, as he here called it, the "Credit Cycle."

The savings-investment analysis first broke in England via the translation in 1924 of Cassel's *Theory of Social Economy*. The first effect was bewilderment, confused nightmares, and intellectual tortures. These mental struggles, groping for a ray of light, brought forth two more or less orderly arrangements of the new pieces of mental furniture so recently imported from Sweden. The brilliant jigsaw puzzles—Robertson's *Banking Policy and the Price Level* and Keynes' *Treatise on Money*—stimulated some hard thinking, though the ideas in both cases were unnecessarily beclouded, dressed up, as they were, in the frightening headgears of Robertson's terminology and the superficially impressive fundamental equations of Keynes.

There can be no doubt that the discussion would have got on faster and would have been on more solid ground had translations of Wicksell's two great books been available, say, about 1920. Believe it or not, the first, and the most important, had already been available in German for more than thirty years when the *Treatise on Money* appeared. The Iron Curtain, let it be noted, is not altogether a new phenomenon.

Unfortunately, Cassel (whose book on its own lines made a great contribution) was a very poor and indeed misleading dispenser of the rich Wicksellian wares. Keynes and Robertson both had only the foggiest idea of what had been going on for thirty years on the Continent. They were grabbing for straws here and there. Keynes refers to Mitchell's "most excellent brief summary," but it can easily be shown that this reliance was a bit shaky, since this summary falls considerably short of presenting an incisive analysis of the great work of the Continental writers. Wicksell is not even mentioned in Mitchell's summary.[9] Keynes, with virtually no firsthand knowledge of Wicksell, contented himself largely with learning what he could (to quote his own words) about "Wicksell's theory in the form in which it has been taken over from him by Professor Cassel." [10] He makes comments about Wicksell (vol. I, p. 197) which would certainly not have been written had Wicksell's books been available in English. Nor would the Gibson wholesale-price–interest-rate relationship have seemed a paradox had he known his Wicksell. Robertson, in his *Banking Policy and the Price Level*, similarly leaned heavily upon Cassel and Mitchell; he acknowledged his obligation to Aftalion and made one or two oblique references to Spiethoff, though he noted that he had never read him.

Writing in December, 1930, on the Great Slump—then only three months old—Keynes said he thought he knew the answer. But one can't help feeling that he was whistling in the dark. He said quite rightly that the trouble is *too little investment*. But why? His answer was woefully weak, revealing his unfamiliarity with the work of the Continental writers. His answer is also weak on consumption. Why did it not take up the slack? Obviously there was much unfinished business to be done—business to which he turned his attention later on in the *General Theory*.

One might be tempted to say, "What a pity that Keynes' mind, from his student days, had not been stocked *at least* with

[9] By 1930 Keynes could indeed have found a good deal in the English language on the Continental writers, but, as Ohlin and Samuelson have said, Englishmen read nothing not printed in England and not even that— Perhaps this is why they have proved themselves to be truly creative thinkers.

[10] See *Treatise*, vol. I, p. 196.

KEYNESIAN THINKING   163

the Wicksellian furniture!" Had this been the case, his *Treatise* sections on investment and saving, instead of being a muddle, might have been a masterpiece. But it may well be that this regret is not well placed. Perhaps the real truth is that his ignorance of Wicksell and other Continental writers, far from being his undoing, was his salvation. Not knowing the Wicksellian answers, he was forced to find his own way about. Lost in the jungle, turning this way and that, at long last he began to find the trails which led to the *General Theory*. Too great skill in handling well-fashioned tools handed down by others may weaken the urge to acquire better tools. No, the *General Theory* might not have been born had Keynes not been so much of an "economic illiterate" that he was compelled to think things through for himself. People overburdened with great learning are often not very creative. Perhaps Pope's famous line "A little learning is a dangerous thing" should be changed to read, "Much learning is a deadening thing."

Under attack Keynes was forced to admit that the fundamental equations of the *Treatise*, and particularly his peculiar formulation of the savings-investment problem, could not stand their ground under scrutiny. By the time he had read the page proofs he already began to have grave doubts. He may even have contemplated ditching the whole thing. In his preface he laid bare the agonizing tortures of an author unhappy over his seven years of hard work.

"As I read through the page proofs of this book [he wrote] I am acutely conscious of its defects. It has occupied me for several years, not free from other occupations, during which my ideas have been developing and changing, with the result that its parts are not all entirely harmonious with one another. The ideas with which I finished up are widely different from those with which I began. The result is, I am afraid, that there is a good deal in this book which represents the process of getting rid of ideas which I used to have and of finding my way to those which I now have. There are many skins which I have sloughed still littering these pages. I feel like someone who has been forcing his way through a confused jungle. Now that I have emerged from it, I see that I might have taken a more direct route and that many problems and perplexities which beset me during the journey had not precisely the significance which I supposed at the time. Nevertheless, I expect that I shall do well to offer my book to the world for what it is worth at the stage it has now reached. . . . I hope to use this experience, which I have now gained, to prepare something on a smaller scale which will try to find the best way to explain the subject. I believe that a right understanding of the topics of this book is of enormous practical importance to the well-being of the world." [11]

Alas, he had in fact not emerged from the confused jungle, as he soon discovered, and the problem was not simply one of an improved exposition. He had still much to learn. But in the meantime he had traversed and retraversed the dangerous pitfalls so often that, once he had worked out the *General Theory*, he had left no important flanks unprotected. He anticipated his critics, as I have shown in my *Guide to Keynes*, at almost every point.

The savings-investment analysis of the *Treatise* was indeed a confused muddle, but some important ideas can nonetheless be salvaged from it. He made a strong effort to differentiate a profit inflation from an income inflation. Actually the differentiation rested on the excess or deficiency of investment in relation to savings as defined in the *Treatise*—a definition which led only into a morass. Nevertheless, there is something to be learned from the concept of a profit inflation or deflation, properly understood, as distinct from an inflation or deflation

[11] *Treatise on Money*, pp. vi–vii.

of the money incomes of employed factors of production. A deflation of the latter (which equates with the costs of production) is a very serious matter, since it involves a general crumbling of the entire cost-price structure. A deflation of windfall profits, however, is really a process of recovering equilibrium in the cost-price structure. A profits deflation is a necessary process of adjustment; an income deflation is a destructive process.

Monetary (and we may add fiscal) policy might appropriately squeeze out a profit inflation. But if we attempted to squeeze out an *income* inflation, the effect would be to produce unemployment. Income stability, i.e., the stability of efficiency wages, is not to be entrusted to banking policy. It must be managed through statesmanlike collective bargaining. This limits sharply the role of the monetary authorities.

The *Treatise* thus aimed, not indeed at price stability, but at the stabilization of the business cycle or the credit cycle, as it was here called. In contrast, both Wicksell and Cassel (who also urged strong central-bank action aimed at price stability) disavowed belief in the feasibility of controlling the business cycle by means of banking policy. Wicksell aligned himself with Spiethoff, who stressed the real factors which control fluctuations in the rate of investment—the essential core, as he saw it, of cyclical fluctuations. Cassel believed that the business cycle was the inevitable concomitant of progress and that this could not and should not be cured by central-bank policy.

In the *Tract*, Keynes had maintained that the essential characteristic of the cycle was a fluctuation, growing out of changing expectations, in the desire of the public to hold cash. In the *Treatise*, it was the fluctuations in bank credit which in turn caused a fluctuation in profits. In the *General Theory*, Keynes shifted to the Wicksell-Spiethoff view that the cycle consisted basically in a fluctuation in the marginal efficiency of capital.

Both Wicksell and Cassel believed, however, that the *long-run, secular* movements of prices were subject to central-bank control. Keynes' *Treatise* maintained precisely the opposite position. It argued that the central bank can and should eliminate the credit or business cycle, but it was not its function to control the long-run trend. To do so would run headlong into collective bargaining, whose proper function it was to stabilize efficiency earnings. If, in fact, following an income inflation, the monetary authorities attempted to deflate prices to their former level, the effect would be a collapse of the newly balanced cost-price structure and with it serious unemployment. Thus the *Treatise* emerged far out of line with both Wicksell and Cassel. The difference is that, whereas Wicksell and Cassel thought that efficiency wages could be controlled through market-demand forces, Keynes believed that in the modern economy a new independent factor was at work, namely, collective bargaining. This position he reiterated in later writings. Finally, at Bretton Woods, the British delegation, which he headed, stood firm on this principle.

The *Treatise*, in its theoretical parts, despite the many rich bits which it offers, must on balance be judged pretty much a failure, except for the sections on index numbers and the technical aspects of banking. As already indicated, Keynes more or less realized, by the time it was first published, that the theoretical sections on saving, investment, and the profit cycle did not rest on secure ground. But there were, nevertheless, innumerable paths in the *Treatise* leading straight to the *General Theory*. And it is this that really makes the *Treatise* important.

C. The General Theory

So at long last we come to the *General Theory*. It is safe to say that no book in the whole history of economics has been subjected to more minute criticism, unless it be Marx's *Das Kapital*. Every effort has been made to discover some flaw which might discredit it. Even minor slips, sometimes inadvertent phrases, have been seized upon as evidence that the whole edifice was about to collapse. What book can anyone name that has been combed as thoroughly for mistakes as has the *General Theory*?

There is a reason for this. Were the book not important, nobody would have bothered. But the book *is* important. It is a challenge. It is a challenge to economic thinking, and it is a challenge to practical policy. It is possibly even more of a challenge to the former than to the latter. And this makes one wonder all the more why the book has generated so much heat.

The book is not an attack on private enterprise. Indeed Keynesian policies have (demonstrably, as far as anything *is* demonstrable in economics) immeasurably strengthened the private-enterprise system. The book is an attack on the belief, so dear to the older school of economists, that the economy tends automatically to function effectively on its own without governmental direction, aid, or support. The independence and freedom of the economic system from politics—this is a tenet deeply cherished by economists and one that many are loath to give up. That the system will not automatically produce full employment—this is something that goes down hard. And in order to preserve this faith, many have been quite willing to save face by arguing that *in the long run*, perhaps even a matter of several decades, this automatic tendency toward full employment is in fact at work. While meaningless and irrelevant in the practical world, it is enough, so some feel, if only the *principle* of automatic self-adjustment can be adhered to. It is surprising how many economists are quite happy if their opponents will only concede that their economic system will perform according to Hoyle even though many of the presuppositions of that system are hopelessly unrealistic and have no bearing on the actual economy which is the object of study and analysis.

The vigor and warmth of the attack on the *General Theory* is all the more strange in view of the undoubted fact that already by the time the *General Theory* appeared the welfare state had been growing ever stronger, and governmental policy was more and more exerting a profound influence upon the economy. *Laissez-faire*, as Keynes had long before pointed out and as everyone was quite aware, was a thing of the past. All modern countries were already a long way on the road toward the mixed public-private economy. Indeed, as some of Keynes' critics are pointing out, all this would have been going on with or without Keynes. Would present-day economic institutions and policies have been very different had Keynes never lived? This kind of question has been asked all through history, and it is just the kind of question that cannot be answered in any convincing manner. Sometimes one wonders what *is* the role of discussion, argument, and debate in the social-evolutionary process. On this question Keynes' mind was quite clear. He was decidedly not an adherent of the materialistic interpretation of history. He believed in the power of ideas. He believed that what he was saying and writing was enormously important; that men's ideas count. He believed that, by taking thought, one can control the course of history.

Keynes' endless agitation for the ideas he believed in throughout the twenties and early thirties was perhaps not responsible for the passing of the gold standard and the achievement of free monetary management. I don't know what is the answer. But there can be no doubt that by the time England left the gold standard in September, 1931, Keynes had profoundly changed the climate of opinion. He had prepared the ground for the general acceptance of the new order, and this general acceptance surely affected its workability. This is of the utmost importance. In similar manner the long and heated debate about deficit financing and the public debt in the United States during the last twenty years has left an imprint on public opinion and political mores which profoundly affects the workability of modern fiscal policy.

Sidney Alexander [12] has put his finger on the vital spot which explains businessmen's aversion to Keynes. An economy operating automatically on its own is one in which business leaders need fear no rivals. A mixed public-private economy is one in which political leaders may more often than not sit in the driver's seat. Business leaders are concerned lest their past undisputed leadership will be permanently challenged. It was this that fanned the flames of opposition to Franklin Roosevelt. The same factors explain the bitter opposition of business and the press to Theodore Roosevelt, who was alleged to be an inciter of class war and a destroyer of business confidence.

Actually, what I have been saying relates primarily to water over the dam. The kind of criticism to which I have alluded is rapidly vanishing. We are living in a mixed public-private economy, and leadership is no longer concentrated in any one sector of the society. The economy in fact is not left to function on its own steam. In the United States, as in other Western countries, political parties vie with each other in proclaiming that the vast powers of the government will be used to the limit to ensure high and stable employment. The conflict with respect to Keynesian policies is for all practical purposes a thing of the past. No sensible person, however, would argue that these policies stem exclusively from Keynes. On the other hand, the effort on the part of some to belittle his towering leadership remains a harmless but ineffective pastime.

So much for the policy aspects. On the scientific plane, how has the Keynesian system stood up? In some quarters it has

[12] *Income, Employment and Public Policy*, W. W. Norton, 1948, pp. 177–198.

become fashionable to say that nearly everyone has accepted the Keynesian terminology but not the Keynesian theoretical analysis. Actually, as one reads the literature one finds that those who use the terminology, whether knowingly or not, in the usual case are also employing the analytical tools of the Keynesian system, sometimes even employing Keynes' tools against Keynes himself!

The Keynesian system is built on the foundation of several specific hypotheses concerning human behavior. Klein, in a recent masterful survey of a vast range of empirical investigations covering all aspects of the Keynesian analysis, concludes that the system is "firmly rooted in fact" and that any reader, whether convinced or not, must at any rate agree that the empirical evidence is not superficial or casual.

The consumption function [13] is, of course, only one of the artillery pieces supporting the Keynesian system. But it has probably been subjected to the heaviest criticism. Discussions relating to the consumption function have, however, by now been pretty much settled—the true meaning of a stable function, the secular upward drift, the long-run ratio of saving to income, the role of external shocks on expectations and short-run shifts in the function, differences in the slope of the function in the downswing compared with the growth phase of the cycle, the impact on the shape and level of the function of recent institutional arrangements such as the built-in stabilizers and transfer payments, and finally the relation of consumption to disposable income and to the national income, etc. Innumerable misconceptions have been cleared up, and in this area I feel that we have reached pretty solid ground. The importance of the subject is attested by the vast amount of empirical work that has already been done, and we can be certain that it will continue to occupy the attention of econometricians for a long

[13] The "consumption function" is a schedule showing the relation of consumption to income at different levels of income.

time to come. In the history of economic thought few instruments of analysis have illuminated the functioning of the economic system so much. Not a few of the puzzles that appear in past literature are cleared up by this very useful analytical device.

This leads me to comment briefly on two lines of attack which continue to interest critics of the Keynesian system. They are: (1) that unless wage rigidity is assumed, the Keynesian system falls to the ground, and (2) the so-called "Pigou effect."

It is sometimes said that the Keynesian explanation of unemployment comes to exactly the same thing as the classical. Under both systems, unemployment, it is said, could not prevail unless wages were kept rigid. Now this statement is certainly in error. The classical system explained that wage flexibility in a perfectly competitive society would surely produce full-employment equilibrium. Keynes explained, on the contrary, that wage flexibility in a perfectly competitive society would produce violent fluctuations of wages and prices —a completely unworkable system. True, he granted the proviso that conceivably there might come by accident a moment when the propensity to consume and the propensity to invest were so perfectly in balance that even a society with wage flexibility and perfect competition might temporarily enjoy full-employment equilibrium. But it would be a highly precarious equilibrium in a changing world where the marginal efficiency of capital does not stay put.

Keynes did not agree with the classicals that a flexible wage system in a competitive society will automatically ensure full employment. He does indeed say that a flexible wage system is one conceivable way to achieve lower rates of interest. So far so good. But his system also shows that a low rate of interest will not *ensure* full employment. Here he differs from the classicists. Moreover, unlike the classicals he was vigorously opposed to the deflation method of achieving low interest rates.

It is of course true that the Keynesian system assumes that wages are *in fact* not flexible in the world in which we live. Economic theory, if it is worth its salt, must deal with the world as it is. It's no use speculating about Mars. In a society in which wages are not flexible the Keynesian system sets out to explain the *level* of income. That level may well be an underemployment equilibrium.

It is not true, however, that the Keynesian system, once wage rigidity is admitted, is nothing else than the classical system over again. True, the classical system, if we assume wage rigidity, admits the possibility of unemployment, but not of underemployment equilibrium. Why not? Because in the classical system, even though wages are rigid, the interest rate will adjust so as to equate saving and investment at full employment. Keynes, however, denied that interest-rate adjustment can be relied upon to equate saving and investment at full employment. Thus the oft-repeated claim that it is all a matter of wage rigidity will not stand up under examination.

And now a word about the Pigou effect,[14] which I once characterized as an "anemic counterrevolution." More than anything else, the Pigou effect has come to be looked upon by Keynesian critics as the all-important thing exposing the flaw in his system. It is sometimes referred to as the "victory" of the classicists over Keynes. But I think everybody, including Pigou, senses that it is an empty victory. Pigou himself has stated that it is only an intellectual exercise with no practical relevance for the real world. The Pigou effect is supposed to occur automatically in a perfectly competitive society with wage flexibility. It is achieved through a process of deflation.

---

[14] The "Pigou effect" refers to the increased propensity to consume resulting from the increase in the *real* value of assets held by the community due to a fall in prices (i.e., to a rise in the value of money).

This is a strange kind of "victory"—a jest, as Samuelson has put it. "The cream of the jest," says Samuelson, "is the final vindication of the classical belief in full employment *by means of a mechanism which leans heavily on indirectly destroying thriftiness and on the matching of full employment saving and investment* so ardently desired by the underconsumption denizens of the academic underworld." [15]

Curiously enough, the Pigou effect argument involves use of one of Keynes' main theoretical contributions—the much-despised consumption function. Sometimes the Pigou effect is even confounded with Keynesian policy. Thus, any positive fiscal-policy program which has the effect of increasing the real value of liquid assets—a policy derived from the Keynesian analysis, is identified with the Pigou effect. Empirical findings with respect to the influence of liquid-wealth holdings on consumption are cited as evidence against Keynes. This, of course, is nonsense. The Pigou effect enters the picture only when a perfectly competitive system with wage flexibility operates, via a process of deflation, to increase the real value of wealth holdings. The Pigou effect, properly defined, has nothing to do with the impact of liquid-asset holdings *as such* upon the propensity to consume.

In conclusion, I am not able to say how far history is changed by new ideas. My philosophy of history is, I confess, not a little foggy. But with respect to the new economy which is unfolding before our very eyes there are some things of which we can be certain. We have achieved a new freedom of monetary management unrestrained by the old gold-standard chains which formerly bound us hand and foot. We have achieved a certain degree of freedom to use fiscal policy unrestrained, at least in considerable measure, by the dogmas of so-called sound finance. These freedoms are of enormous importance for the successful workability of the system of

[15] David McCord Wright (ed.), *The Impact of the Union*, p. 336.

private enterprise. Without these freedoms the future would indeed be dark. I am not able to measure with mathematical accuracy the weight of Keynes' influence on these developments. But we do know that he spent his life brilliantly pleading these causes. We know that people listened. We know that he drew blood. We know that he stirred up a great controversy.

A good Marshallian like Pigou did indeed, in his *Economics of Welfare*, ably rationalize much of the welfare state which had already by 1920 been firmly incorporated into the social structure. But in the more usual case, Marshallian economists, especially in the United States, could be counted upon to show ten good reasons why any proposed reform, whether guarantee of bank deposits or social security, was unworkable and would likely do more harm than good. Franklin Roosevelt, with his socially inventive mind, was always on the lookout for economists who could tell him how a thing that *needed* to be done *could* be done. But for the conservative man of affairs in the heyday of laissez-faire capitalism Marshallian economics was highly useful as a resistant to social change.

One thing is certain. The old orthodox economics left economists completely unprepared to cope with the problems of the Great Depression. In the blackest days of that devastating cataclysm Professor Taussig, one of the most forward-looking of the old school, made a nationwide radio address which it was my good fortune to hear. One felt that here was a great man struggling to pierce the darkness around him. The speech was anything but dogmatic. We just don't understand, he said, very much about the problems created by the great catastrophe. We don't really know what to do. Listing some of the New Deal proposals (which to most intellectuals seemed completely "cockeyed," as indeed some of them were), Taussig suggested that it might well be better to try something than to do nothing, and perhaps we had better try a little of several of the more promising suggestions. It was a candid talk by an honest man who did not shrink from disclosing to the world the bankruptcy of the old economics.

Within the last few decades the role of the economist has profoundly changed. And why? The reason is that economics has become operational. It has become operational because we have at long last developed a mixed public-private economy. This society is committed to the welfare state and to full employment. The government is firmly in the driver's seat. In such a world, practical policy problems became grist for the mill of economic analysis. Keynes, more than any other economist of our time, has helped to rescue economics from the negative position to which it had fallen to become once again a *science* of the Wealth of Nations and the *art* of Political Economy.

APPENDIX

WOODROW WILSON
AS AN ECONOMIC REFORMER[1]

Woodrow Wilson, as an economic reformer, drew heavily upon the ideals of Jeffersonian democracy. Wilson was very much a Jeffersonian liberal. Indeed, no small part of his economic program fitted into the pattern of nineteenth-century liberalism, using that term in its French meaning. But he did not stop there. Important segments of his program prepared the way for later and more far-reaching reforms.

Wilson's early life was spent in a rural environment which reflected the Jeffersonian agrarian and individualistic philosophy. Growing up in the home of a scholarly minister and a university-trained mother, and devoting himself to a life of learning, he had perhaps more points of resemblance to the quiet, cultivated intellectual that Thomas Jefferson was than any other American President. In his background, in his character, in his outlook on life, Wilson was in every way a true Jeffersonian.

The agrarian democracy of Jefferson was, however, by the time Wilson entered politics, on the way out. The period around 1910–1914 marked, in truth, the end of an era. By 1910 nearly 10 per cent of the American population lived in great cities of a million or more inhabitants, and 25 per cent lived in cities of over 75,000. The strictly rural population had fallen

[1] Lecture delivered at the Harvard University Memorial Celebration in honor of Woodrow Wilson, March 13, 1956. Reprinted from Autumn, 1956 issue of the *Virginia Quarterly Review* with consent of the Editor.

from 95 per cent in Jefferson's day to 50 per cent in Wilson's time. Of the total gainfully occupied, urban workers constituted 45 per cent when Wilson became President, while farmers and farm laborers constituted only 33 per cent, and the urban middle classes composed of professional people, small businessmen, and salaried employees constituted around 20 per cent. Urbanization, together with a highly concentrated industrialism, was surging ahead, submerging the old rural individualistic society—a society in which every enterprising young man could look forward to becoming an independent entrepreneur, owning his own farm or running his own small business.

Only a few years before Wilson's inauguration as President the country had witnessed the vast merger movement of 1898–1904 in which more than 300 consolidations had been formed, controlling 40 per cent of manufacturing capital and creating something skirting on monopoly or near monopoly in over 70 leading industries. Five million immigrants had entered the country in the five years preceding Wilson's inauguration as Governor of New Jersey, and they continued to enter at the rate of a million a year during his two years as governor and his first three years as President. The Anglo-Teutonic ethnic character of the American population was rapidly changing. Urbanization, industrialization, and immigration set in motion new political pressures and social upheavals. The great body of middle-class Americans were becoming increasingly concerned lest plutocracy and mass industrialization might undermine the individualistic character of their democracy.

By the time Wilson arrived on the political scene the country had already witnessed more than a quarter-century of Populist and agrarian agitation.[1a] Our political controversies today, bitter and emotional and often unscrupulous as they are,

[1a] Cf. Richard Hofstadter, *The Age of Reform*, Alfred A. Knopf, 1955.

seem nonetheless somewhat tame compared with the excoria-
tions heaped by the Populists and muckrakers upon trusts,
plutocrats, and the so-called "barons of industry." At the turn
of the century Theodore Roosevelt, though bred and reared in
an elite and cultivated class, had hurled blistering denunciation
at the "malefactors of great wealth."

As professor and university president, Wilson's lot had been
cast with the "able, the well-born, and the rich." In this capacity his sympathies were neither with the Populist orators nor
indeed with the new leaders of wealth and power—crude, uneducated, and corrupt as they often were. Wilson's sympathies
lay rather with the old elite middle class—college-bred, with
family background, steeped in traditions of idealism and high
moral values. His economic philosophy before he entered politics was, like that of most academic men of his time, based
largely on book learning without much vital touch with the
actual world about him—an economic philosophy of *laissez
faire*, with primary emphasis on so-called sound money and
free trade. His political philosophy concerned itself first and
foremost with honest and efficient government. But the role
of government, as he then saw it, involved little of a positive
character. He was indeed at that point of his career a true
Jeffersonian, both in politics and in economics.

Considering this background, together with the firmness of
his convictions and the age at which he entered politics, the
transformation which occurred in his social outlook, his economic philosophy, his attitude toward trade unions and labor
legislation, toward Populist ideas and programs of reform, is
nothing short of spectacular. The like of it cannot be found,
as far as I am aware, in any other major political figure in
American history. As a practicing politician he flung aside
mere abstract thinking and quickly sensed the realities of
economic life in a rapidly changing world.

When Wilson was nominated for governor of New Jersey

in 1910, Bryan's influence in the Democratic party, having suffered defeat three times, was highly tenuous. The conservatives in the party were again back in the saddle. Most of Wilson's friends were conservatives. Yet no sooner had he become a candidate for governor than he cast his lot with the wave of progressive thinking which, while indeed on the march, was far from strong enough to give any secure promise of victory.

No one acquainted with Wilson's earlier career could possibly, I think, have foreseen this metamorphosis. And this is particularly true when we consider that characteristic of inflexibility which is typically attributed to him. Once he became a practical politician he adjusted with amazing flexibility to the realities confronting him. He became quickly aware of the ominous changes in the industrial and social life of the nation and the need for new and positive institutional reforms. The new wine needed new bottles. Wilson was indeed no revolutionist. He was essentially a conservative reformer. Suitable adjustments, he believed, could be made within the framework of the existing social order. But if these adjustments were not made, the American democratic ideal was, he became convinced, in peril.

As professor and university president he had not been drawn into the new movements. Indeed he looked upon most of the agrarian and Populist agitation as pure demagoguery. Yet when he became an active politician, he picked out what seemed useful and forged it into a workable program of reform. His leadership, during his first administration, distilled the best and sanest of the radical thinking of his time into law.

The groundwork for the Wilsonian reforms, to which I shall refer in greater detail in a moment, had indeed been laid in the turbulent twenty-five or thirty years which preceded his inauguration. Here we find the antecedents of his principles and his programs.

The mugwumps [2] of the eighties, intellectual elites, including Henry and Brooks Adams and other solid and substantial New Englanders, stood for honesty, integrity, and efficiency in government. They stood for reform in political morals, not reform in the social structure. At the opposite pole were the Populists, Greenbackers, Silverites, and Western Agrarians. They fought, to be sure, as did the mugwumps, the prevailing graft and corruption, but they went deeper. The social order, they believed, was fast tending away from a rural democracy to a centralized system controlled by a small clique of industrial magnates and so-called financial barons. The structure of society had to be reformed, so they believed, before there could be any fundamental reform in political morals. In this they differed from the mugwumps. The citadels of power had to be wrested from the special interests and a people's government restored. Thus the Populists attacked the giant trusts, demanded strict regulation of the railroads and a Federal income tax as means of leveling down the power of the growing crop of millionaires—a new phenomenon in American life. Honesty and integrity could never be achieved, so they believed, unless the concentration of power was struck down at its roots. With a score or more of millionaires in the United States Senate, they called for the election of senators by direct vote of the people. They portrayed the country as rapidly becoming a nation consisting of two classes—the rich and the poor.

The agrarian and Populist movements, often demagogic and sometimes hysterical in tone, made their appeal primarily to desperate farm debtors weighed down by impossible mortgage burdens in the face of falling prices and to urban workers whose strikes against long hours and incredibly harsh working conditions often ended in rioting and open violence.

[2] Mugwump, meaning in Algonquian "great man," and used in New England to describe self-conceited politicians.

Nothing would have come, however, of all this bluster and talk had there not in fact been going on a revolutionary change in the structure of the American Economy. It was this solid fact, which no amount of wishful thinking could dissipate, that led later to the Progressive Movement—a movement which found practical expression in the political leadership first of Theodore Roosevelt and later of Woodrow Wilson, and which was sustained and nourished, not by pockets of Populist revolt, but by an alert and fairly prosperous middle class.

The Progressive Movement of Teddy Roosevelt and Woodrow Wilson, be it noted, blossomed not in the midst of hard times, falling prices, and widespread unemployment. It flourished in the great period of expanding prosperity from 1900 to the First World War. The movement was the product, not of bankruptcy, mortgage foreclosures, wage reductions, or unemployment. It sprang from a growing awareness on the part of a large proportion of Americans that a profound change was taking place in the social and economic structure, and that this transformation was affecting the nature of government itself.

On the wave of rising prices and growing profits, the great merger movement of 1898 to 1904 had run its course. The middle class was alerted to the danger of monopoly, of government's becoming a mere tool of big business, of concentration of power and wealth in the hands of a few. Many of the alarmist phases of the Populists now began to sound more sensible— true descriptions of a revolutionary change in the social structure which no man with open eyes could any longer ignore. Sensible people began to fear that a plutocracy might supplant the democracy. Teddy Roosevelt made speeches on the "Cure of the Disease of Wealth." He thundered against the "predatory interests," the purblind folly of the very rich, their greed and arrogance. The fight was on. Leading papers in the industrial and financial East denounced him as an inciter of class war, and they pointed with alarm to the effect of his speeches on business confidence.

As President, Theodore Roosevelt accomplished one thing which, for that period, was supremely important. He gave the people a new sense of pride and confidence in their government. He made them feel that government was, if not superior to, at least able to stand up and talk back to big business. It was this, above all, that made him popular. It was not what was actually accomplished, whether in the anthracite coal strike settlement or the Northern Securities case, that mattered. It was the fact that he, as President, dared to stand up and pit the government against the great business combinations, and in particular against those individuals who had come to be known in the popular mind as the "malefactors of great wealth," a phrase coined by T. R. himself.

Without Roosevelt we might not have had the Wilson reform movement. Yet there was a difference. Roosevelt saw the true trend of the modern industrial evolution. He saw that it was not possible to turn the clock back to a truly competitive system. Big business was here to stay. You would destroy the gains of modern technology if you broke up large units. The government must indeed be a match, and more than a match, for big business, but it must not be anti-big-business. T. R. charged, though I believe not quite fairly, that Wilson was trying to reestablish an outmoded laissez-faire economy in which competition, not government regulation, was counted upon to ensure a well-functioning society.

Teddy Roosevelt was prepared to sanction large organizations not merely of capital but also of labor and farmers. He looked to organizations of farmers, and to the Federal government itself, as counterpoises to big business. He was fifty years ahead of Professor Galbraith with his doctrine of "counter-vailing power."[3] The government was to be on the job twenty-four hours of the day. To trusts and monopolies he hung out the sign: "Thus far shalt thou go but no farther." Government control rather than the restoration of an outworn competition was his motto. His was not a "one-act show," namely, to break up monopoly and then withdraw from the stage. Government had, in his view, a full-time job—a job which could not be left merely to the free play of market forces.

It was into this atmosphere of Rooseveltian reform and reconstruction, silhouetted against the background of the reactionary Taft Administration, that Woodrow Wilson stepped when he was nominated for governor of New Jersey. As I have already indicated, plunged into the realities of prac-tical politics, he quickly sensed the need for fundamental reform. He was indeed, as T. R. had charged, in favor of the utmost restoration of competition, yet he also recognized that large-scale organization of business, up to a certain point, was a normal and inevitable development. He did indeed stress the role of competition, and rightly so, but it is not true that his program consisted merely of a restoration of a competitive regime of *laissez faire*, as Teddy Roosevelt had charged. Wil-son in fact did more than Teddy himself toward building into the social structure new strong governmental institutions quietly but continuously at work strengthening and invigorat-ing the economy.

Wilson laid, as I shall show in a moment, a number of foundation pillars that proved later to be essential under-pinnings for the New Deal reforms of our own day. An insti-tution which characterizes in a highly significant manner our present-day economic structure is that of collective bargaining.

[3] Cf. J. K. Galbraith, *American Capitalism, The Concept of Counter-vailing Power*, Houghton Mifflin Company, 1952.

It would be difficult to point to any part of our social structure which lends greater strength to our modern democratic institutions. Sound industrial relations constitute a vital part of the modern welfare state. Wilson's contribution to the development of a sound system of collective bargaining was very great. The skeptic may indeed point to the fact that the courts quickly emasculated the hoped-for Magna Carta of labor—the anti-injunction provisions of the Clayton Act. Viewed from the longer run, it doesn't matter. Labor won, not in the courts indeed but in the eyes of the American people and in the eyes of Congress, a new position before the law. It could henceforth claim that the American people had given it a new status. The legalistic view that labor is a *commodity* placed trade unions indeed technically on an equal status with other litigants; but it amounted *de facto* to gross *inequality*—a point elaborately documented by Brandeis both before and after he ascended to his place on the Supreme bench. Wilson's Clayton Act set the stage, true though it be that the drama was not completed until at long last legal opinion was decisively changed as a result of the Supreme Court fight in 1937.

The welfare state is preeminently a large disburser of funds, partly in the form of transfers between groups within the entire economy—an equalizing process—and partly in the form of grants to state and local governments, also in large part an equalizing process. Wilson's Administration gave us the Smith-Lever Act, which matched state funds dollar for dollar in the promotion of agricultural extension work. Similarly it gave us the Federal Highways Act, which also matched state funds dollar for dollar. These were small beginnings, but they established a principle of far-reaching importance—a principle which radically altered the role of the Federal government. Wilson put the Federal government firmly in the saddle. It was he who swung the Democratic party away from its states'-rights tradition. From these basic beginnings the Federal government was later to become the all-powerful instrument of a welfare state.

Thus far I have cited two important foundation stones in the building of the welfare state, namely, collective bargaining and the equalizing fiscal operations of the Federal government. This latter—the Federal government as dispenser of funds—could never have assumed any significant role had the taxing powers of the Federal government not been greatly enlarged. Wilson's Administration gave us the personal income tax. Credit for this belongs, of course, to a large number of individuals, notably Cordell Hull, but also to continued agitation going back to the early Populist and Progressive Movements. Without Wilson's reform Administration, however, the harvest might not have been gathered. But it is safe to say that no one then, Wilson included, had any conception what a powerful engine for later New Deal fiscal policy had been created.

Equally important for modern fiscal policy is the Federal Reserve System. Modern fiscal policy rests basically on two pillars: (1) the vast powers of taxation represented by the progressive income tax and (2) the power of money creation and monetary management represented in the Federal Reserve. Wilson's Administration gave us these two foundation pillars of modern fiscal policy, powerful instruments of the welfare state. Keynesian economics, it may be added, has taught us how to use them.

Thus Wilson went far beyond the negative policy of merely trying to restore competition. In fact, the direct results of his efforts to restore competition were meager indeed. The Underwood tariff, designed to increase foreign competition and weaken monopoly power, was quickly nullified by the war and soon thereafter by Republican legislation. The Clayton Act was largely nullified by the courts, but also by the flow of events. The war had demonstrated beyond doubt the efficiency of big business and the dependence of the economy upon large-scale organization. The country awaited with bated breath the decision of the Supreme Court in the United States Steel case of 1920. There was, I think it is fair to say, general approval of the decision, which was favorable to the steel company. Destroying an efficient organization would simply paralyze the industries of the country. Theodore Roosevelt's view, not Wilson's, became the dominant one. Still, the Sherman law and the Wilsonian amendments remained on the books, and it would be a gross error to call them a dead letter.

The productive efficiency of large-scale business is, however, one thing; the frenzied finance and wild speculation associated with the great merger movement of 1898 to 1904, and again the widespread merger movement of the fateful twenties, are quite another thing. The New Deal has largely accepted the view that large-scale operations may be necessary to achieve efficiency. The New Deal, however, centered its attack on the financial manipulations in the capital market— evils of long standing, but peculiarly conspicuous in the twenties. There followed the notable reforms of the Securities Act of 1933, the Securities Exchange Act of 1934, and the Holding Company Act of 1935. Monopoly and unfair practices remain indeed the concern of the Federal Trade Commission (a Wilsonian institution) and of a somewhat revitalized Anti-trust Division. In this area we are perhaps still "playing by ear" and are so far only moderately satisfied with the results. But in the field of financial reform we have achieved notable progress. The early bitter opposition to these reforms has been converted by now into virtual universal approval.

Wilson could not have foreseen the superstructure which was to be built upon the foundation which he laid, and could he have done so, he might well have disapproved, as seen through *his* spectacles, of many of the New Deal reforms. But he was not unaware that his program involved far more than the erection of what we would today call an Hayekian liberalism. His program involved not less government but more government. It involved a renaissance of popular government, an ousting of big business from the seats of political power. Wilson threw his weight against the great concentration of industry and finance represented by Morgan and others who personified in the public eye this concentration of power. He demanded a new respect for government. He wanted the government to become an instrument for the public good, not a tool of uncontrolled private capitalism or, to use his own words, "privileged big business." He wanted to bring the forces of the whole people once more into play. We need, he asserted, a new method, a new spirit, a new *renaissance* of democratic ideals, a program of far-reaching reform, but accomplished within the framework of the existing social order.

Using, in some measure, the rhetoric of Jefferson, he went nonetheless far beyond the Jeffersonian conception of the role of government. Sensitive to the powerful flow of events, which Jefferson could not foresee, Wilson saw that democracy could not survive in a laissez-faire uncontrolled private capitalism. Urbanization and modern industrialism rendered the people helpless in a society which accorded to the state only the powers of police protection. The government belonged to the people. Instead of an instrument of oppression (a conception of the state carried over from the days of absolute monarchy) the state was the only means by which a democratic people could find a solution for the problems created by urbanism and industrialization. Wilson and Jefferson were indeed kindred spirits, and if they could have met across the span of time, would doubtless have found much in common. Fundamentally their ideals were the same. But Wilson, especially after he was plunged into practical politics, saw very clearly that the Jeffersonian ideals could not be implemented in the modern world by the methods suitable to Jefferson's time. Jeffersonian government applied to the conditions of the twentieth century would have made a mockery of Jeffersonian ideals. There are indeed among us today plenty of that kind of fake Jeffersonians, but Woodrow Wilson was not one of them. It is not the outward form but the unseen substance of Jeffersonian thinking that counts. Sensitively aware of the realities about him, Wilson, as an economic reformer, was indeed a true Jeffersonian in that he applied Jeffersonian ideals in a constructive and realistic manner to the problems of his time.

In line with this view of Wilson's economic thinking I close with the following rather long quotation from his *New Freedom:*

"I feel confident [said Wilson] that if Jefferson were living in our day he would see what we see: that the individual is caught in a great nexus of all sorts of complicated circumstances. The program of a government of freedom must in these days be positive, not negative merely. We stand in the presence of a new organization of society.

"We have changed [he continued] our economic conditions, absolutely, from top to bottom, and, with our economic society, the organization of our life. The life of the nation centers upon questions of the very structure and operation of society itself, of which government is only the instrument. We are in a temper to reconstruct economic society, as we were once in the temper to reconstruct political society. We stand in the presence of a revolution—not a bloody revolution —but a silent revolution. Some radical changes we must make in our law and practice. Some reconstructions we must push forward, which a new age and new circumstances impose upon us. The whole stupendous program must be publicly planned and canvassed. The laws of this country have not kept up with the change of economic circumstances. . . . If you do not adjust your laws to the facts, so much the worse for the laws, not for the facts, because law trails along after the facts."

In these words Wilson revealed his kinship with Jefferson, but he also disclosed his faith, that changed economic conditions demand fundamental positive reforms—reforms that go far beyond what is encompassed in the label "a Jeffersonian Democrat."

INDEX

191